Keeping up the Kardashian Brand

Keeping up the Kardashian Brand

Celebrity, Materialism, and Sexuality

Amanda Scheiner McClain

LEXINGTON BOOKS
Lanham • Boulder • New York • Toronto • Plymouth, UK

Published by Lexington Books
A wholly owned subsidiary of Rowman & Littlefield
4501 Forbes Boulevard, Suite 200, Lanham, Maryland 20706
www.rowman.com

10 Thornbury Road, Plymouth PL6 7PP, United Kingdom

British Library Cataloguing in Publication Information Available

Library of Congress Cataloging-in-Publication Data
McClain, Amanda Scheiner, 1979-
Keeping up the Kardashian brand : celebrity, materialism, and sexuality / Amanda Scheiner McClain.
p. cm.
Includes bibliographical references and index.
ISBN 978-0-7391-7715-0 (cloth : alk. paper) -- ISBN 978-0-7391-7716-7 (electronic)
1. Keeping up with the Kardashians (Television program) 2. Fame--Social aspects--United States--History--21st century. 3. Television personalities--United States. 4. Celebrities--United States. 5. Branding (Marketing)--United States. 6. Social media--Economic aspects--United States. 7. Popular culture--Social aspects--United States. I. Title.
PN1992.77.K445M33 2014
791.45'72--dc23
2013022295

ISBN: 978-1-4985-2061-4 (pbk)

For Jordan and Jasper

Contents

Chapter One

The Family and the Business

The Kardashians are more than just a reality TV show: they are a contemporary cultural touchstone, recognizable throughout the world; connoting warrantless celebrity, voluptuous beauty, and a flash-in-the-pan marriage. The Kardashians are prevalent not only on television, but throughout the media landscape. The appellation appears extensively in the mainstream press, recurring in seminal newspapers and tabloid magazines alike. Their faces regularly adorn magazine covers and their names are common in gossip columns. Various family members promoting sundry projects are featured regularly on early morning and late night television. Additionally, the Kardashian family members often appear in assorted media; for example, Khloé Kardashian co-hosted the 2012 reality competition program *The X Factor*. Similarly, the mother of the Kardashian clan, Kris Jenner, is scheduled to host her own television talk show. Venturing into film, Kim Kardashian appeared in a Tyler Perry movie, *Temptation: Confessions of a Marriage Counselor*. Moreover, Kim's pregnancy and delivery of critically acclaimed musician Kanye West's child facilitated even more media presence. As Robin Roberts declared on *Good Morning America*, "you cannot escape the Kardashian phenomenon" (2011). On her namesake program, Barbara Walters (2011) elaborated upon their ubiquity and image: "The Kardashians are everywhere, their empire endlessly self-replicating with spin-off after spin-off, a strange mix of trashy sex, upscale excess . . . tabloid melodrama and suburban family life." Furthermore, the family members avidly utilize social media, documenting the minutia of their lives through words and photos, as well as networking with fans and other celebrities. In short, the Kardashians are omnipresent, permeating contemporary American culture.

The varied Kardashian media products are worthy of study for their prevalence in entertainment media and their relevance to American life. This book attempts to make sense of the Kardashian celebrity and brand empire by systematically examining the flagship reality program *Keeping Up with the Kardashians*, family members' social media utilization, and the family's popular press presence. This holistic case study of Kardashian media permits insights into contemporaneous American culture, namely societal norms, values, and ideologies. Via examination of family, relationship, and gender benchmarks throughout media, as embodied by one intensely popular family, we may obtain myriad insights into American culture on individual and universal levels. Furthermore, a structural analysis of how the Kardashians attain cultural relevance through sundry types of media is important. Marketing and business models are emerging that address the need to strategically utilize both stratifying and coalescing forms of media. This work addresses the structural and cultural elements in formation and sustenance of a successful brand through the blending of old and new media. Thus, this book adds to the case studies of brands' utilization of traditional and social media's intersection, while concurrently examining cultural significances within the brand.

Mediated popular culture offers a portal of analysis for American culture. Through the lens of media, we learn about our peers, our society, and ourselves. Moreover, portrayals of societal standards illustrate how American culture is supporting or modifying traditional American ideologies, such as capitalism and individualism, as well as the separation of the public and private spheres historically denoted by gender. While the civil liberties of women and other groups have steadily improved over the last century, the examination of prevailing attitudes as depicted by the Kardashians, in conjunction with the concurrent media criticism, indicate a disconnect between reality TV participants and their fans, and those who critique and review them in media. Finally, the Kardashian brand signifies a cultural fascination with wealth, beauty, celebrity, and ourselves, cyclically bolstering the fortunes of the Kardashians.

KARDASHIAN BACKGROUND

According to their own publications, in 1978 Kris Houghton joined the Kardashians, a wealthy Southern-Californian and Armenian family, by marrying Robert Kardashian, Senior (1944-2003). Over the course of seven years, Kris and Robert Kardashian had four children: Kourtney, Kimberly, Khloé, and Robert, Jr. The children had a privileged and family-oriented upbringing, replete with expensive cars, horses, ski and beach vacations, and over-the-top birthday parties, including Kim's fourteenth birthday party held at Michael Jackson's Neverland Ranch. Their Beverly Hills house had a pool and tennis courts; neighbors included Bruce Springsteen and Jay Leno (Kardashian et al., 2011). Their glamorous lifestyle included celebrity friends like Nicole and O.J. Simpson. During the infamous O.J. Simpson murder trial, Robert was a member of O.J.'s legal defense team, becoming a household name during this time period. Robert and Kris divorced in 1991, and within a year, Kris married Olympian decathlete Bruce Jenner, who had four kids of his own, including reality show *The Hills* participant Brody Jenner. This marriage produced two more daughters: Kendall and Kylie.

Middle-sister Kim claimed that her divorced parents were amiable during her childhood: "On Father's Day, my mom would cook Bruce and my dad breakfast and we'd do holidays together" (de Bertodano, 2011). In their autobiographical book, *Kardashian Konfidential*, the sisters aver, "family values were always so important in our family. In a weird way, the divorce actually strengthened them for us" (Kardashian et al., 2011, p. 28). Likewise, attributing their strong work ethic to their family background, the sisters assert, "we may have been spoiled, but we weren't brats!" (Kardashian et al., 2011, p. 40). They reiterate, "Both of our parents were so strong on family values and confidence, and emphasizing responsibility and the importance of hard work" (Kardashian et al., 2011, p. 117). Of course, statements from their own works pandering to the public must be taken with a grain of salt; the family may strive to reach the largest audience by adapting their personal histories to match public sentiment.

Along with being supposedly family-oriented, the Kardashian upbringing was strict. The sisters claim that as teens they had an early curfew, weren't allowed out Saturday nights, and were required to attend church services on Sunday mornings. Khloé and Kim rebelled; Kim by eloping for a short-lived marriage at age nineteen and Khloé via experimenting with alcohol. Their parents did give each a car (Kim and Kourtney received BMWs, Khloé a Mercedes), however, "we had to sign a contract saying we would keep up our grade average in school, that we'd wash the car and take care of it and pay for our own gas" (Kardashian et al., 2011, p. 39). The sisters were informed they'd receive no parental financial help after finishing their educations. The only sister to complete college is Kourtney, who graduated from the University of Arizona in 2002.

The Kardashian sisters describe their childhood as religious. Not only did they attend a local Presbyterian church throughout their childhoods, but when Kris felt a connection to a particular pastor, she eventually founded a church, installing him as the spiritual leader (Kardashian et al., 2011). The Life Change Community Church, led by Pastor Brad Johnson, is a recipient of 10 percent of Kim Kardashian's income and an unspecified amount of Kris Jenner's (Magrath, 2011).

Throughout their upbringing, the importance of beauty was emphasized. According to *Kardashian Konfidential*, Kris Jenner began waxing her daughters' eyebrows once they reached age eleven and taking each to a salon for bikini-line waxing at age thirteen (2011, p. 36). She also treated her daughters to weekly manicures and pedicures. The curvy sisters also placed an importance on body image throughout their teen years. According to Kim, "I was insecure when I was younger . . . sometimes I didn't feel skinny enough" (Kardashian et al., 2011, p. 90). The significance of beauty and body ideals is highly evident in their adult lives as well, as manifested throughout the television series.

Before reality TV stardom, the three older sisters held various jobs, some entrepreneurial in nature. As teens, Kim and Khloé both worked for their father's business, while Khloé also worked as a personal assistant. Later, Kim worked as a closet organizer, eBay seller, and stylist, and Kourtney and her mother co-owned a children's clothing store named Smooch, which operated for six years, 2003-2009 (Kardashian ct al., 2011). This experience led to the three sisters opening their women's clothing store, DASH, in 2006.

A year later, the February 2007 release of Kim's pornographic sex tape vaulted Kim into the mainstream spotlight, which she had courted for years as a friend of Paris Hilton. This explicit video, ostensibly recorded for private use, starred Kim and Ray J, the brother of 1990s singer Brandy. Kim sued Vivid Entertainment, the video's distributor, settling for $5 million dollars (de Bertodano, 2011).

In October of 2007, *Keeping Up with the Kardashians* debuted and was immediately popular, spawning the spin-offs *Kourtney and Khloé Take Miami*, *Kourtney and Kim Take New York*, and *Khloé and Lamar*, among others. The shows feature the family members living their lives and "being themselves." As the sisters state in *Kardashian Konfidential*,

> We are businesswomen, sisters, a mother, a wife, entrepreneurs, fashion designers! (Though Kim has dabbled in acting.) And we didn't set out to be celebrities. We're just living our lives, and our claim to recognizability is that we do it in front of the cameras, and people like watching it" (Kardashian et al., 2011, p. 107).

While they realize their claim to fame is "being themselves," they contend work must be done to sustain fame and its effects. They assert, "being a celebrity is a job. And like any job, it has its downsides . . . because if you fall into the trap of taking yourself too seriously, you risk getting a very swollen head" (Kardashian et al., 2011, p. 131). The glamorous situations, celebrity friends, and exotic locales evident in their televised lives, engendered tautologically by their fame, may contradict this down-to-earth attitude given lip service.

Keeping Up with the Kardashians **Popularity**

The Kardashians achieved their fame primarily through a reality show portraying the daily mundanity and foibles of a large, zany family's life, teeming with five sisters, one brother, parents, boyfriends, and friends. *Keeping Up with the Kardashians* is intensely popular; the highest-rated series ever on the E! channel, and broadcast in over 150 countries around the globe (Jenner, 2011). According to Kim, the idea of a reality show originated from family friend Kathie Lee Gifford, "Whenever she came over, she'd be like, 'Where are the cameras? You guys are a reality show'" (de Bertodano, 2011). After shooting an informal pilot, a mutual friend (Deena Katz, casting director for *Dancing With The Stars)* secured a meeting between Kris Jenner, Ryan Seacrest, and his producing partner, Eliot Goldberg. Kris pitched a family-focused reality show able to reach audiences of all ages, as correlated to the various life stages of family members. Moreover, Kim had recently become fairly well known, due to her sex tape and friendship with Paris Hilton. Ryan Seacrest, Bunim/Murray Productions, and E! bought Kris's pitch and a month later, *Keeping Up with the Kardashians* went into production (Jenner, 2011). On *Nightline*, Kourtney described their shooting schedule as "eighteen hours per day, six or seven days week" (McFadden, 2010).

Since debuting in 2007, the TV program *Keeping Up with the Kardashians* has grown immensely in popularity and ratings, raking in profit and fame for the family. The first season averaged more than one million viewers per episode and "together with repeats, drew an audience of more than thirteen million during its first four weeks" (Newman & Bruce, 2011, p. 3). Later seasons averaged more than three million viewers per week (Reinstein, 2010), ranking it more popular than basic cable shows such as *Mad Men* and *American Horror Story*. Indeed, *Keeping Up with the Kardashians* is the highest-rated series ever on the E! cable network; its fifth season debuted with over 4.5 million viewers (Jensen, 2010) and ended with 4.7 million viewers tuning in for the season finale, a record for E! (Merkin, 2010). In season six, a two-part bridal special, titled *Kim Kardashian's Fairytale Wedding*, attracted 4.2 million viewers for the E! channel over consecutive nights (Stelter, 2011). The program appeals to a certain specified audience in particular, as 1.1 million women ages eighteen to thirty-four watched the season six finale, setting an E! channel record for that particular demographic (Fernandez, 2011). In 2012, more than 1.5 million women aged eighteen to forty-nine watched the seventh season debut (E! Entertainment, 2012). The show performs well "because they are fun to watch and the family is relatable. The public enjoys the aspirational intimacy" (Piazza, 2011, p. 102).

The ancillary spin-offs are also well-liked. The second-season debut of the 2009 *Keeping Up with the Kardashians* spin-off, *Kourtney and Khloé Take Miami*, earned over 3.5 million viewers (O'Leary, 2010), while its finale earned 3.7 million viewers (Jensen, 2010). The first season of the next series in their reality franchise, *Kourtney and Kim Take New York*, debuted in January 2011 to over 3 million people (Wheeler, 2011). In November 2011, over the course of two days, 10.5 million viewers watched the two-part special, *Kim Kardashian's Fairytale Wedding* (Goldberg, 2011). The concluding episode of season two of *Kourtney and Kim Take New York*, which portrayed Kim and Kris Humphries' brief marriage, garnered a season-high of 4.5 million viewers. This season finale ranks as the third most watched telecast in E!'s history (Levine, 2012). In fact, E!'s top three highest-rated telecasts are all Kardashian episodes; the top-rated broadcast is the season four *Keeping Up with the Kardashians* finale while the second-highest rated is the *Keeping Up with the Kardashians* fifth season premiere (Rice, 2010). The cumulative programs' popularity demands study of the intrinsic meanings within the Kardashian family.

The E! network—which green-lit the production of *Keeping Up with the Kardashians* and continues to broadcast the myriad Kardashian series—is one of the niche cable channels directed primarily at women and teens. According to the advertising industry, women are responsible for eighty-five percent of household purchases (Lotz, 2006, p. 28). E! represents the expansion of targeting specific women, a consequence of the proliferation of cable channels and the need for highly-specified audiences. This narrowcasting to certain audiences results in more channels and programming directed at women, fostering the ascendance of female-centered dramas. Moreover, determining programming for particular pinpointed demographic groups permits for the creation of "distinct narratives that resonate with that group" (Lotz, 2006, p. 27). The Kardashian programs and shows of its ilk are representative of this genre of female-oriented production and scheduling. By 2011, on Sundays, the day *Keeping Up with the Kardashians* aired, E! jumped among women aged eighteen to forty-nine from being ranked thirteenth in the ratings to number one (Piazza, 2011, p. 102). According to Lisa Berger, E!'s Vice President in charge of Original Programming, "It [*Keeping Up with the Kardashians*] has changed the face of E!" She continued, "We were a place to report on celebrity; we weren't a place to break and make celebrity, which is now the whole idea of the E! brand" (Newman & Bruce, 2011).

In April of 2012, Kris Jenner inked a deal with E! earning the family $40 million dollars for the seventh, eighth, and ninth seasons of *Keeping Up with the Kardashians* (Villareal, 2012).

Branding Empire

While Americans may watch television for entertainment and information purposes, it primarily exists in order to earn advertising dollars and funnel profits to creators and parent companies. The ubiquitous commercials, product placements, and endorsements bolster the American culture of conspicuous consumption. Indeed, "entertainment, advertising, and consumerism have operated hand-in-hand since the very earliest years of the medium" (Curtain & Shattuc, 2009, p. 2). The Kardashian family is an exemplar of this entertainment, advertising, and consumerism confluence on a multimodal scale, utilizing television, social media, and journalism to create and sustain celebrity. Moreover, they actively encourage commercialism, which in turn helps sustain their merchandise empire. The Kardashians embody the transparent embrace of the consumerism intrinsic in contemporary culture, brashly relying on reality-TV-produced celebrity and the confessional, no-holds-barred nature of reality television to sell themselves and branded products. Their intense cross-platform self-promotion works; the family earned an estimated $65 million in 2010 (Newman & Bruce, 2011). Newman & Bruce (2011, para 5) contend that the Kardashians have a:

> wholly modern business model for making money. It's one that emphasizes accessibility [and] harnesses three commercial components: fan interaction via social media (the family has a collective thirteen million Twitter followers); best-selling products and brand endorsements; and, of course, that hyper-successful reality franchise.

All three of these elements are intricately and symbiotically intertwined, with the program *Keeping Up with the Kardashians* at the center of the money-making web. While the family members earn $20,000 per episode, the program is "merely a vehicle to promote the Kardashian brand and sell its many products" (Piazza, 2011, p. 102). The family's greatest asset is "a business model that uses *Keeping Up with the Kardashians* as a hub for all [the] family's other business ventures. It is a centralized distribution system through which the family sells products, stories, and themselves" (Piazza, 2011, p. 99). The family realizes this, noting, "the popularity of our shows on E! has led to all sorts of ventures—our own clothing line, jewelry, fragrance, diet supplements, skin care, just to name a few" (Kardashian et al., 2010, p. 213). *Keeping Up with the Kardashians* is "a perfect commercial for our products" (Kardashian et al., 2010, p. 214). The exposure is worth much more than the payment for the show. For the Kardashians, "business strategy has always been brand first, fame second" (Piazza, 2011, p. 103). The family is unsurpassed at the many techniques of monetizing reality fame (Newman & Bruce, 2011).

Stemming from the television series, "their brand extensions . . . comprise the heart of the family's enterprise" (Newman & Bruce, 2011, para 8). The family commands a "branding empire that includes fashion boutiques, fitness videos, credit cards, a best-selling fragrance, skin care products, and a self-tanner" (Wilson, 2010, p. 1). Their revenue stream includes book sales, media and appearance fees, television revenues, endorsement deals, and product sales (Piazza, 2011). The family has had endorsement deals with Sketchers, Tropicana Juicy Rewards, and Carl's Jr., along with a myriad of other companies.

Not only are they paid to publicly endorse products, they have a stake in the development and sales of many products, such as skin care line Perfect-Skin, diet and nutrition supplement business Quick Trim, and the Kardashian-branded fragrances, among others (Jenner, 2011).

However, their primary ventures are fashion-oriented. At various points, the sisters have had a clothing line with Bebe, a swimwear line with Beach Bunny, a clothing line for QVC called QVC-K-Dash by Kardashian, and the Kardashian Kollection for Sears, comprised of clothing and accessories (Kardashian et al., 2010). By August 2010, The Kardashian Kollection included the plus-size Kardashian Kurves line (Gormish, 2012), comprised of clothing in sizes 18 to 24, as well as the Kardashian home line, available at Sears. As of fall 2012, through a collaboration with licensee Jupi Corp. and British apparel entrepreneur Philipp Green's Arcadia Group, the Kardashian Kollection was offered in thirteen countries, through U.K. Dorothy Perkins' boutiques and in-store shops within British department store BHS. Consumers in the U.K., Turkey, Kuwait, Thailand, Israel, Qatar, Malaysia, Bahrain, Saudi Arabia, the United Arab Emirates, Indonesia, Singapore, Australia, and the Philippines were able to buy the clothes, which are all priced under $100. As of 2013, the Kollection will be available in Brazil, Russia, and China (Tran, 2012a). Kris Jenner also has her own clothing line sold exclusively by QVC, the Kris Jenner Kollection (Jenner, 2011). The list of merchandise seems to grow daily, and includes a lifestyle store in Las Vegas, Kardashian Khaos (Jensen, 2010). The three older sisters jointly own three Dash clothing boutiques, one each in L.A., Miami, and New York City.

Besides fashion, literature is another domain in which the family partakes. Kourtney, Kim, and Khloé received a $150,000 advance for *Kardashian Konfidential*, a lifestyle book cowritten by the sisters. Released in December 2010, it has sold a minimum of 275,000 copies (Piazza, 2011, p. 101). A fictional book cowritten by the sisters, *Dollhouse*, released in November 2011, is presumed to have merited a similar advance, plus a portion of sales. The *New York Times* noted celebrities typically receive advances of $200,000 to $1 million (Bosman, 2011). Kris Jenner also released a book, *Kris Jenner and All Things Kardashian*, in October 2011. Additionally, the two youngest sisters, Kendall and Kylie Jenner, are publishing their first novel in 2013. Published by Karen Hunter Publishing/Gallery Books, part of the Simon & Schuster publishing house, the young adult fictional book features two sisters on an adventurous journey (Finlayson, 2012). At the time of its release, Kendall and Kylie will be 17 and 16, respectively. In the process of publicizing their books, various family members continue to appear throughout media.

Kendall and Kylie, the youngest siblings, have their own miniature version of a branding empire, which contributes to the larger Kardashian cache. In 2011, the sisters announced a jewelry line collaboration with Pascal Mouawad and his Glamhouse jewelry collection (which also houses Kim's jewelry line) (Apatoff, 2011). That line is targeted to "girls twelve to nineteen" with prices "between $20 and $60" (Apatoff, 2011). In 2012, the sisters became *Seventeen* magazine's "West Coast fashion contributors, for which they select their favorite trends every month" (Orenstein, 2012). Last but not least, in 2013 the sisters designed a juniors' fashion line consisting of "T-shirts, pants, shorts, and accessories," produced in conjunction with textile and apparel manufacturer Majestic Mills (Tran, 2012b). Not only does this increase the family's revenue, but also potentially introduces the brand to a younger audience.

Importantly, "positive media impressions drive the Kardashian brand" (Piazza, 2011, p. 104). Measuring media impressions is a public relations technique to determine the number of times a brand or celebrity is mentioned in the mainstream press and social media. The more the Kardashians appear in media, the more popular their brand appears. The family reaps rewards for mediating their family milestones and personal appearances. Kourtney's first pregnancy story and photographs sold to *Life & Style* magazine as a package deal for $300,000, which included multiple stories: "the pregnancy announcement, sex of the baby, birth announcement, first baby photos, and body-after-baby reveal" (Newman & Bruce, 2011). A 2013 *US Weekly* cover featuring Kourtney's baby weight loss earned her a reported $200,000 (Garvey et al., 2013). Family members also earn money from personal appearances: Kim's personal appearance fee is between $100,000-$250,000 dollars domestically and up to $1 million dollars abroad (Newman & Bruce, 2011). The venues hosting the appearances benefit from the publicity as well. However, the Kardashians profit in other ways, as Kim explained in *Cosmopolitan* magazine:

> The appearances are good moneymakers. And they're also a great way for me to connect with people in places like Oklahoma, where I would never go otherwise. Those girls going to the clubs will be buying my perfume (Piazza, 2011, pp. 101-102).

As a *New York Times* article noted, "ultimately, what Ms. Kardashian and her sisters create and sell are products based on their own image" (Wilson, 2010, 1). This project seeks to understand how this money-producing image is constructed and the significances that reside within it.

Kim Kardashian

Middle-sister Kim, arguably the most famous, is nearly omnipresent; she is featured in her family's reality TV show, its spin-offs, appears regularly in tabloid magazines and on fashion magazines covers (and on a 2009 *Playboy* cover), makes personal appearances, has an iPhone app, and constantly updates her Twitter stream. Between 2008 and 2012 Kim appeared in many television shows, including appearances on *America's Next Top Model*, *How I Met Your Mother*, *Last Man Standing*, *CSI: NY*, and *Drop Dead Diva*, as well as participated in *Dancing With The Stars* and *The Celebrity Apprentice* (Jensen, 2010). She also appeared in the 2013 Tyler Perry movie, *Temptation: Confessions of a Marriage Counselor*. Moreover, her child with popular musician Kanye West guarantees her place in the media spotlight for several more years.

Kim has effectually converted her fame into a revenue-producing brand. In 2010, she earned an estimated yearly income of $7 million (Reinstein, 2010). The following year, Kim reaped a reported $18 million profit from her wedding special (Piazza, 2011). Fox News estimated her 2012 net worth to be $35 million dollars (McKay, 2012).

Despite her entrance to the public landscape through a sex tape, Kim "stands out for the fact that she is generally still regarded in a positive light by many consumers" (Wilson, 2010). In fact, regardless of "the lurid sex tape and the photo-shoot for *Playboy*, Kim manages to peddle a prudish image, disliking alcohol and finding her sisters' clowning and partying exasperating" (de Bertodano, 2011). Kim's image is that of a

> . . . sexy good girl. Kardashian does not drink to excess, does not do drugs, and doesn't party. In order to strictly control her image, she will not be photographed at a club unless she is being paid to appear at that club and even then she will be out of there before midnight and exercising early the next morning (Piazza, 2011, p. 103)

The "sexy good girl" is apparently well-liked by consumers. An issue of *Shape* magazine featuring her on the cover was its best-selling issue of 2010, her *Allure* magazine cover ranked as its third-best-selling issue of the year, and her nude turn on the cover of *W* magazine was its second most popular issue of the year (Newman & Bruce, 2011). She has been a spokes model for Bongo Jeans, Sketcher's sneakers, Midori Liquor, Sugar Factory candy stores, and other consumer products. Kim's commercial for fast-food restaurant Carl's Jr. "generated 258 million media impressions (the number of times the ad was viewed or mentioned in the media), more than three times the quantity achieved by any of the chain's previous celebrity commercial stars and more than all of them combined" (Piazza, 2011, p. 100).

Author Piazza contends Kim has become "a brand by virtue of a continued assault on the consumer market through the entertainment news media" (2011, p. 92). Kim Kardashian, the brand, sells not only other companies' products, but her own as well. In February of 2010, Kim released her eponymous fragrance; it became national beauty chain Sephora's top seller of the year (Newman & Bruce, 2011). As of July 2012, three fragrances have borne Kim's name. Khloé and Lamar also have their own fragrance, *Unbreakable by Khloé and Lamar*. A special edition of this fragrance, titled *Unbreakable Joy*, was released for the 2012 holiday season. Kim is also the "cofounder and chief fashion stylist for ShoeDazzle.com," a website that "gives members access to a celebrity stylist" to help them choose the appropriate shoes, jewelry, handbags, and apparel for their personal style (Tschorn, 2010). In 2010, Kim expanded her plethora of business roles, earning a $180,000 fee for executive-producing reality-TV program *The Spin Crowd*, starring her friend Jonathan Cheban. *The Spin Crowd* was the highest performing show in its 10:30 pm E! time slot (Piazza, 2011, p. 101).

As the amount of business ventures might indicate, Kim is often depicted in her family's series as industrious. *The Spin Crowd* (and frequent guest star on *Keeping Up with the Kardashians*) Jonathan Cheban expressed,

> She is the busiest woman I have ever met, and yet once the show started, she was out promoting it on the *Today* show and on Twitter. She never flakes on you. That's what sets her apart. Her business model is about morals and standards, never screwing anybody and never flaking (Piazza, 2011, p. 101).

Kim, when asked about her success, stated, "it's just a lot of work that goes into this whole thing that might not be so visible to the public eye. I think hard work pays off, and I think having a strong work ethic. No matter what, we have to stay focused" (Piazza, 2011, p. 103). The Kardashian shows transparently depict this "hard work." However, what the Kardashians and their friends consider work, others may not. Kris Jenner facilitates the ostensible work of creating and sustaining celebrity.

"Momager" Kris Jenner

Kris Jenner has been described as a "branding mastermind" (Newman & Bruce, 2011) and as unquestionably "the wizard behind it all" (Piazza, 2011, p. 93). Kris combines her roles of mother and manager into her literally trademarked title of "momager" (Jenner, 2011). She describes her job as "creating, nurturing, and juggling the insanely busy careers, endless personal appearances, and business enterprises" of her family (Jenner, 2011, p. viii). Kris manages the entire extended family, including son-in-law Lamar Odom, a professional basketball player, earning ten percent of each member's income for her work (Esmalian, 2010). The management job combines aspects of public relations and sales, pushing the family into the spotlight. Kris herself noted that she never expected that her family would become an "entertainment empire" (Jenner, 2011, p. 211). As momager, Kris oversees a global brand, which often requires the conflation of her mom and manager roles.

According to Kris, a former American Airlines flight attendant, her career began by working in her grandmother's and mother's candle shops in upscale San Diego as a teen (Jenner, 2011). In her book, *Kris Jenner . . . and All Things Kardashian*, she claimed that helping in their shops instilled the value of hard work within her. Growing up, Kris's family was dominated by her grandmother. Kris later replicated this matriarchal structure: "In my family, if the matriarch says something is okay, then it is okay" (Jenner, 2011, p. 16). Kris rules not only the private home, but the public business as well.

According to her own publicity, Kris's entertainment career commenced upon her 1991 marriage to Bruce Jenner. Bruce had achieved fame for his gold-medal performance in the 1976 Olympics and then embarked upon minor race car driving and acting careers. By the time of their marriage, his fame had faded, something Kris worked to rectify. Bruce noted, "When I met her . . . she was just a little Beverly Hills housewife, but packed inside her was an entrepreneur" (Merkin, 2010, para 4). In 1991, Kris claims she said to Bruce, "There should be Bruce Jenner clothing, Bruce Jenner exercise products, Bruce Jenner endorsement deals, Bruce Jenner vitamin supplements. We'll build this house one speech and one endorsement at a time" (Jenner, 2011, p. 113). She created a press kit and highlight reel, selling Bruce as a motivational speaker and product endorser. Eventually, "the speech requests started rolling in, the business changed, we upped his fees, and we got him back on the road again" (Jenner, 2011, p. 114). By 1994, Bruce was presenting motivational speeches to Fortune 500 companies like Coca-Cola. That year, Bruce and Kris created and promoted a series of popular infomercials for gym equipment: *Super Fit with Kris and Bruce Jenner*. The infomercials aired in 17 countries, up to 2,000 times a month (Newman & Bruce, 2011). Kris also amplified her profile by briefly working as a correspondent for the ABC daytime talk show *Mike & Maty* in the mid-1990s (Newman & Bruce, 2011).

While Kris is the matriarch of her family, her dual role as mother and manager doubtlessly influence her personal relationships with family members. The daughters express, "Having a momager definitely muddles things a little . . . the times we don't communicate well are when we're speaking to our manager and she's reacting as our mom" (Kardashian et al., 2010, p. 119). Of course, miscommunications aren't always the momager's fault: "we probably yell at her more easily because she's our mom. We trust her more than we would a regular manager, but we wouldn't get so intense with someone else. Sometimes it's tricky having a momager, but we wouldn't want it any other way" (Kardashian et al., 2010, p. 119). Kris labels her role as more than manager and mom, but as "a producer, a manager, a negotiator, a publicist, a business manager, a stylist, and at times a caterer and set decorator" (Jenner, 2011, p. 267).

Kris parlayed fifteen minutes of reality TV fame into a plethora of business ventures and endorsements. She partially accomplished this by partnering with other successful enterprises. For example, the family and GNC collaborated on the creation of the Quick Trim vitamin and weight loss supplement line (Jenner, 2011). The line debuted in 2009 and as of 2011, had earned over $45 million in sales (Newman & Bruce, 2011). Similarly, Kris aligned with Lighthouse Beauty to create a signature fragrance for Kim, which she later did for Khloé and Lamar as well. The fragrances sell at mass retailers such as Macy's and Target. The sisters also designed a makeup line in association with Boldface Licensing, Khroma Beauty, which is sold at Ulta beauty stores. The line's marketing is aided by "behind the scenes tips provided by the Kardashians and their makeup artists via Twitter and YouTube" (Boldface Licensing + Branding, 2012). Under Kris's guidance, a skin care line was developed, PerfectSkin, for which the family recorded an infomercial (Jenner, 2011). She has also formed partnerships with Sears, QVC, and nail polish brand OPI, among others.

Kris allegedly sorts through at least ten endorsement offers per day (McFadden, 2010). In another example, she spearheaded a multimillion-dollar deal for Kim to represent Sketchers sneakers (Newman & Bruce, 2011). In yet an additional successful commercial affiliation, Kardashian Khaos, a lifestyle store that exclusively sells Kardashian-branded lifestyle merchandise, opened in the Las Vegas Mirage casino. The store carries "products that the Kardashian girls and Kris Jenner own, represent, market and endorse, coupled with exclusive Las Vegas souvenir items." Items sold in the boutique include: "t-shirts, novelty gambling chips, a surprise beach towel, playing cards, private label makeup by Stila, and individually designed scented candles from each girl and Kris" (www.mirage.com, June 6, 2012).

In a rare misstep, Kris engineered a deal with financial service companies Mobile Research Card and Revenue Resource Group to launch the Kardashian Kard, a prepaid credit card aimed at teens. The Kardashians were to receive "$3 for every card activated or sold, 25 percent of fees, a $75,000 advance on royalties and a $37,000 signing bonus" (Newman & Bruce, 2011, p. 5). However, after then-Connecticut Attorney General Richard Blumenthal criticized the card's predatory fees, Kris pulled out of the deal. The Kardashian Kard, directed at the teen fans, "cost $99.95 to own, including a $9.95 fee to buy the card and additional monthly fees of $7.95" (Singletary, 2011, para 2).

Kris's own career has grown exponentially in tandem with her daughters'. In 2008, when Kim appeared on *Dancing With The Stars*, Kris was a special correspondent for *The Insider* and *Entertainment Tonight* (Jenner, 2011). Kris has appeared on myriad talk shows and magazine covers hawking the Kardashian brand created through her business ventures. In 2010, Kris partnered with music management group Wright-Crear Management for a short period of time, managing the all-female pop group BG5, as well as employing her son Rob within the company (Ross, 2010). By 2012, she had partnered with renowned music producer Babyface, expanding her potential music-related business (S7, E4).

CONCLUSION

The Kardashian family is everywhere. They are a conspicuous and overexposed element of contemporary American culture, yet there is a significant lack of academic research devoted to this phenomenon. Through studies of the structural use and content of diverse media, such as the namesake TV series, social media, and ancillary press coverage, this project reaches distinctive conclusions about the ideals and paradoxes inherent within Kardashian brand.

Unlike in academia, much has been written about *Keeping Up with the Kardashians* in the popular press. An article in *Entertainment Weekly* noted that the show adheres to a tried and true sitcom formula: "Whereby lapses in judgment or boneheaded mistakes lead to nutty conclusions and hurt feelings that get resolved with confession, discussion, apology, and hugging" (Jensen, 2010, p. 46). The same article called it a "conventional family sitcom, once you get past the booze, bleeped language, and bawdy sex talk" (Jensen, 2010, pp. 43-44). Ted Harbert, president and CEO of Comcast Entertainment Group, called the show "a modern-day *Eight is Enough*" (Jensen, 2010, p. 44). Are these claims correct—is the show an innocuous family-friendly sitcom-esque show? While this may be at least partially true, the themes within the series and other media controvert this supposition.

This book interrogates the popular press's family-friendly claims via a systematic exploration of narratives depicted on the popular and provocative show. In sum, examining the *Keeping Up with the Kardashians* television series, social media use, and contextual press coverage illuminates the meanings that reside with the presented images. Media analysis helps illuminate contemporary societal norms.

First, through a discourse narrative analysis of *Keeping Up with the Kardashians*, I discover the inherent themes and contradictions within the series narratives. On *Keeping Up with the Kardashians*—and throughout other media—the Kardashians exploit sexuality to gain publicity and celebrity, while both supporting and challenging traditional gender roles and other conventional standards. An overriding ideal throughout the assorted media is materialism and concern about status. Moreover, throughout these dichotomous values, an emphasis exists on the conflicting roles of women, beauty standards, and fame.

Secondly, I closely examine Kardashian interactive media practices, investigating how the Kardashian family members' social media usage affects their celebrity and brand. The Kardashians avidly utilize social media to refine, manage, and promote their image. How do the Kardashians manipulate social media and audiences to preserve and augment celebrity and in turn, monetary value? An analysis of the intricate relationships between new media and celebrity sheds light on the production and maintenance of the Kardashian brand.

Finally, I examine popular press interpretation of the family itself, exploring what the coverage of the Kardashian family connotes about contemporary American culture. What does criticism of the Kardashians imply about American cultural norms as understood by journalists? This last study reveals contemporary reactions to the family and their celebrity, underlying themes throughout the reporting, and the role journalism plays in constructing and supporting fame.

THIS BOOK

The following two chapters contain an analysis of the first seven seasons of *Keeping Up with the Kardashians*. This study is grounded in the fields of television studies and celebrity, finding several dualities presented in the program: family/business, traditional/untraditional gender roles, intimate/ transgressive family, beauty/unhappiness, narcissism/celebrity, and overt sexuality/conservatism. Chapter 3 also includes an examination of series themes, all of which pertain to materialism, discussed in relation to the theoretical concept of conspicuous consumption.

In chapter 4, I appraise literature connecting the research areas of celebrity and new media. These are traditionally considered two separate subjects, yet an emerging field of study examines how the two intertwine. The subsequent study explores the contemporary interaction of celebrity, new media, and commerce through a narrative analysis of Kim Kardashian's social media presence; initially through analysis of her Twitter use, and subsequently via analysis of her blog. All of the Kardashians maintain highly "followed" Twitter accounts, frequently update blogs and Facebook pages, and utilize other social media, such as Kendall and Kylie Jenner's Instagram account. On Twitter, Kim Kardashian is immensely popular; according to the *New York Times*, she is ranked sixth in popularity and ninth in influence (Leonhardt, 2011). Her blog is also extremely popular, receiving over 40 million hits per month (Newman and Bruce, 2011). Kim Kardashian embodies the intersection of two different online worlds: the seemingly pointless babble of social media and the commercialism of online consumerism and advertising. Her embrace of social media helps generate and sustain her fame and fortune.

Chapter 5 is an analysis of Kardashian press coverage. This study examines popular press (newspapers, magazines, television, etc.) through a Newspapers Plus database search of the summer of 2011—June 1st through August 31st. This research contextualizes the Kardashians in time and place, reveals public opinion, and explores media themes, particularly how media both uphold and reject the family-constructed Kardashian image. Additionally, this investigation illustrates how media understand, explain, and help buttress Kardashian celebrity. In sum, this chapter explores how mainstream journalism reacts to and contributes to American cultural mores.

Chapter 6 is comprised of a summary of each study's conclusion, a discussion of findings, and a triangulation of the studies' results, engendering an extrapolation of particular ideas inherent within the Kardashian media empire. Ideals and themes found across varied media are significant and evocative. Moreover, this conclusion includes a discussion of the Kardashian prominence in contemporary culture, as well as societal meanings within Kardashian media. Finally, this last chapter discusses ideological implications of the Kardashian brand's capitalization upon the amalgamation of celebrity and new media, resulting in amplified celebrity and economic success.

While social media and press coverage are important to examine, television is still the most utilized American medium. As of 2008, every hour spent watching video online was matched by fifty-seven hours spent watching television (Stelter, 2008). Many of these hours consist of reality TV. The Kardashian presence on television, online, and throughout the mainstream news media is investigated by the qualitative method of narrative analysis.

METHOD

Narrative analysis is a detailed textual reading methodology, illuminating cultural mores and paradoxes through both narrative form and content. Across history and time, people have come to understand their worlds through narratives. Modern narrative study derives from the field of structuralism, building upon the work of Vladimer Propp, Roland Barthes, and Ferdinand de Saussure, among others. Their work determined how the organizational structure of a narrative can infer meaning; this narrative structure can be applied to myriad forms of discourse (Herman, 2007, p. 5). As Barthes (1977) noted, signs within stories are encoded with wide societal meaning. Thus, narratives provide the structure of meaning conveyance. Narratives are a means of learning and teaching (Berger, 1996) as well as a means of representation and explanation (White, 1987). Narratives encode values and model behaviors; they help consumers understand reality (Bird & Dardenne, 1988). White (1987) asserts narratives connote ideology through epistemic choices and suppositions. Every closure-providing narrative is attached to its own set of ideals; as such, "narrativizing discourse serves the purpose of moralizing judgments" (p. 24). Moreover, as they are widely superficially understood, narratives are used to maintain hegemony (Gramsci, 1971).

Subfields of narratology include feminist (e.g., Page, 2007), rhetorical (e.g., Phelan, 2007), and ideological (e.g., Herman & Vervaeck, 2007). Feminist narratology seeks to focus upon "forms and functions of women's narratives" (Page, 2007, p. 190). Rhetorical narratology focuses upon the event of the narrative itself and the relationships between teller and audience, concentrating upon "an ethics of the told and an ethics of the telling" (Phelan, 2007, p. 203). Ideological narratology is primarily concerned with the interpretation of ideological concepts within narratives. Ideology is defined as "a body of norms and ideas that appear natural as a result of their continuous and mostly tacit promotion by the dominant forces in society" (Herman & Vervaeck, 2007, p. 217). Television narratives often include codes that refer to ideologies (Fiske, 2000). The following analysis applies components of all three of these narratology subfields to television, digital, and press narratives. Within the varied Kardashian media I examine narratives, the dialogue and means used to convey story and meaning, and interpret implicit ideology. However, in order to accomplish this analysis, various terms must be identified, defined, and elucidated.

Narrative is "a basic human strategy for coming to terms with time, process, and change" (Herman, 2007, p. 3). Bal (2009) breaks down narrative into three elements: the narrative text (or the discourse), the story (the content of the text) and the fabula, or actions. Stories are "accounts of what happened to particular people—and of what it was like for them to experience what happened—in particular circumstances and with specific consequences" (Herman, 2007, p. 3). Within the story is the fabula, a "series of logically and chronologically related events that are caused or experienced by actors" (Bal, 2009, p. 5). Discourse is the "presentation and reception of these events in linguistic form" (Bridgeman, 2007, p. 53).

Herman elaborates, contending that core elements of narrative include:

> (i) structured time-course of particularized events which introduces (ii) disruption or disequilibrium into storytellers' and interpreters' mental model of the world evoked by the narrative . . . conveying (iii) what it's like to live through that disruption, that is, the 'qualia' (or felt, subjective awareness) of real or imagined consciousness undergoing the disruptive experience (2007, p. 9).

In other words, a narrative is chronological, contains an element of conflict, and explains what it's like to live within the narrative. All stories and thus narratives must contain a chronological element; without the time element, a story becomes a description.

Narratives therefore take place sequentially, and "the past, present, and future of a given event or action affect our interpretation of that action" (Bridgeman, 2007, p. 52). Time and space are more than necessary background, rather "affecting our basic understanding of a narrative text" (Bridgeman, 2007, p. 52). Every story also necessarily includes a conflict, or an interruption in equilibrium that propels the action or plot.

Finally, a narrative must be rooted in the human experience. This is necessary to impart meaning and significance into a story, as the relating and comprehension of the narrative are both human activities (Page, 2007).

The narrator is the person relating the story. The narrator may be a main character, or possibly an external narrator: the person behind the camera. The identity of the narrator influences the composition and content of a text by contributing his or her perception (Bal, 2009). This is termed focalization, or how the narrator's worldview colors communication to audiences (Bal, 2009). Focalization is thus "the relation between the vision and that which is 'seen,' perceived." The narrator presents "a point of view, a certain way of seeing things, a certain angle, whether 'real' historical facts are concerned or fictitious events" (Bal, 2009, p. 145-146). For example, when Kim Kardashian provides her version of events in a confessional narrative to the camera, the audience is able to comprehend a story from her perspective. Kris Jenner may provide a secondary focalization upon her turn to speak.

Narrative and discourse analysis may be conducted of literature, prose, journalism, speech, dialogue, and also of digital media and television. The principles delineated here will be applied to multiple formats; however, much of the research concerns televised narratives.

Television Narrative

Television is "America's central institution for storytelling" (Thorburn, 1988, p. 63). It is a "cultural forum" resplendent with narratives that help maintain the status quo, even while polysemic (Newcomb, 1988). Within television content, narrative and rhetorical elements serve as familiar storytelling techniques (Silverstone, 1988).

Television texts and the structure of television are interrelated; televised narratives have their own particular set of parameters. Television narratives must work within the industry's constraints; shows are generally designed to last thirty or sixty minutes and to incorporate advertising disruptions (Mittell, 2007). For instance, an hour-long program is designed to have four acts replete with climaxes, broken up by commercial breaks (Thompson, 2003).

Commercial-free programs, often aired on subscription-based cable networks like HBO, also adhere to a typical two or four act structure dependent upon program length, although not as rigidly. Moreover, several plot lines featuring varied characters provide the feeling of consistent action and increased realism (Thompson, 2003). Other structural factors may include adjusting stories due to actors' needs, fan reactions, or network mandates (Mittell, 2007).

Butler (2006) contends a televised narrative within a serial program has seven clearly defined elements: multiple protagonists, exposition, motivation, narrative enigma, cause-effect chain, climax, and resolution (or lack thereof). Together, these elements relate a story. Within television narratives there is a defined set of characters; each enables varied plot lines (Butler, 2006). These characters also explain the action (exposition) and reveal why these actions occurred (motivation). Narrative enigmas are the questions driving the story: what will happen? The cause-effect chain refers to the constant commercial interruptions, resulting in teasers to keep the audience interested over the break. A climax is a culmination of a plot line; however, rarely do these lead to a complete series resolution. Rather, the ultimate resolution of a series is deferred until the series finale, if at all. Resolution is rarely offered, as the desire for satisfactory ending keeps viewers habitual.

Another particular parameter of narrative television is its open-ended nature; many series promulgate a continuous story for several episodes (Feuer, 1986; Mittell, 2007). This contrasts with a film or novel, which typically has a concise ending point. Within a series, episodes may contribute to an overall mythology or help create a world particular to the series, yet each episode typically consists of a finite story unto itself (Mittell, 2007). There may be an overarching season-long narrative and/or a closed narrative in each episode. For example, each episode of *The Simpsons* adds to the knowledge viewers have of Springfield and the world the Simpson family and friends inhabit, yet each episode stands alone as well. The resolution of each episode provides a return to equilibrium (Mittell, 2007), or banality of normal existence. However, serial dramas are typically more open-ended, with stories that transcend single episodes. Such serial narratives are typically more concerned with changes to characters' relationships than events that occur (Mittell, 2007). Television narratives also usually occur in parallel to real-time, as opposed to movies, where years may be compressed into hours (Fiske, 1987). This aids in audiences perceived relationships with television characters (Fiske, 1987).

Characters are integral to television narratives. Characters rely on codes of meaning to clarify personality attributes (Butler, 2006). These meaningful codes resonate with dominant culture (Fiske, 2000) and thus are easily understood by the majority of audience members. Codes include a character's race, physical appearance, sartorial style, and other attributes. Contextual knowledge of previous media experience is also engaged while ascertaining character qualities (Butler, 2006). Furthermore, production elements such as lighting, editing, and actor performance affect character development (Butler, 2006).

Television genres often have their own intrinsic norms, a certain style or order of events (Mittell, 2007). For example, reality-TV narrative norms typically include a confessional break in action, when a subject speaks directly into the camera and thus the audience. The audience must interpret these narrative norms and modern TV conventions into an order to create a mental narrative: "fragmented camera shots, multiple streams of auditory material, and conventions of visual composition . . . turning them into a story that typically appears 'realistic'" (Mittell, 2007, p. 167). As viewers watch, they learn and comprehend the story as communicated through filming conventions, dialogue, genre, character arcs, codes, patterns, and action events. This learning process allows "for more complex and sophisticated narratives to emerge and achieve mass popularity" (Mittell, 2007, p. 170).

Reality television, while encompassing the aspects of narratives delineated above, also often includes an overt narrative: the confessional, in which a participant speaks directly to the camera, typically relating his or her version of a plot point, and including his or her emotional reaction. As Curnutt noted, this reality-TV convention for participants is "a reflexive dialogue about their time on the show through to-camera monologues and interviews" and is used for "character development and plot fabrication" (2009, p. 254). These "first-person" narratives often conflate the demarcation lines between participant and viewer (Dovey, 2000). The reality TV viewer is treated as a participant, a cherished confidant, which also functions to reveal more insight into the speaker. This confessional draws viewers in and is a unique feature of reality television, drawn from its documentary forefathers.

Moreover, certain ideals are often present within the structure of television narratives. These include echoing off-screen norms, such as importance of masculine ideals and the happiness of the conventional nuclear family (Feuer, 1986), or possibly patriotism, celebrity, capitalism, and the American dream of success (McClain, 2011).

Television, which reaches large audiences through industrial practices and contains broadly sweeping narratives, is one of the institutions that sustain the American status quo. Social media, while much more new, also functions to sustain American ideologies. Within social media, our "everyday communicative/representational practices are structured by the social order, by larger systems of belief, and by hierarchies of knowledge" (Thurlow & Mroczek, 2011). Thus, it is imperative to study myriad forms of media. This book focuses upon the meanings inherent within discourse and narratives, while also taking into account medium-specific limitations.

Chapter Two

Family, Gender, and Transgressions

The twenty-second-long *Keeping Up with the Kardashians* opening credits feature the family jostling and squabbling in front of a city facade. Within this introduction, family members display the traits they continually exhibit throughout the series. First, Kris asserts her dominance within the family hierarchy by rearranging her daughters' positions and ordering Bruce to change his clothes. Khloé drolly asks if the wind machine is necessary, marking herself as the funny sister. Kourtney assertively speaks to someone off camera, establishing her place as the oldest, bossy sister. Rob, smiling, appeals to his sisters to make him laugh. This plea is indicative of Rob's constant need for guidance and dependence upon others. Next, Kris asks where Kim is, and another family member answers that Kim is always late, displaying her disregard for others' time. Finally, Kim rushes into the scene, wearing a tight-fitting red dress, and poses sexily, hand on hip, in front of the whole family. Her forefront placement signifies that she is the star of the show, the celebrity, while her family members' expressions of disgust convey their thoughts about her vanity and conceit. Their opinions clearly show on their faces, promising a series inclusive of indecorous and impolite behavior. Throughout the entire sequence the audience sees flash bulb explosions, hears recognizable camera clicking noises, and views photography equipment, connoting celebrity status and fame. Everyone is attired in flashy clothing, demonstrating wealth; the women wear sequined dresses and animal print, while the men are attired in button-down shirts and nice slacks. Finally, Kylie, age 11, pulls a golden cord which sends the backdrop to the ground, revealing the idyllic Jenner home in Calabasas, California. The audience literally sees what is behind the curtain: the ostensibly real life of the Kardashian/Jenner family.

Keeping Up with the Kardashians follows the blended Kardashian/Jenner family, focusing on mom and stepfather Kris and Bruce Jenner, and Kris's adult children, Kim, Kourtney, Khloé, and Rob Kardashian. Kris and Bruce's teen daughters, Kendall and Kylie Jenner, also appear. Various boyfriends and friends pop in and out, notably Kourtney's boyfriend, Scott Disick, and in later seasons Khloé's husband, Lamar Odom. Each show typically features some sort of family or business dilemma, and often a conflation of both.

For this analysis, I watched all the episodes within the first seven seasons of *Keeping Up with the Kardashians*. Season one contained eight episodes and season two consisted of ten, each approximately twenty-two minutes long. Season three lasted twelve episodes, each about twenty-two minutes in length. Seasons four and five were comprised of eleven episodes. Of the season four episodes, four were approximately forty-two minutes long and seven were twenty-two minutes in length. The season five episodes were all about twenty-two minutes long, except the season finale, which was forty-two. Season six consisted of thirteen episodes, of which two were forty-one minutes long and eleven were approximately twenty-two minutes, while for season seven the amount of episodes upped to eighteen, each approximately forty-four minutes long. Seasons eight and nine are airing in 2013 and 2014 (Villarreal, 2012).

Conducting the narrative analysis within each episode and of the holistic series, I examined the discourse, the story, and the fabula, or actions. Within these overarching narrative elements, both verbal and visual, I predominantly took notice of patterns and themes. Of a particular significance here was the overt focalization established by the confessional narratives, or when each family member spoke directly to the camera and thus the at-home audience, providing plot exposition and supplementing story arcs through explanation of motives and emotions. This permitted characters to fully explain, and occasionally redeem themselves, particularly the Kardashian sisters and mother. Here, the series is considered through a television studies theoretical framework.

TELEVISION STUDIES AND GENDER

As Butler (2006) noted "television remains the principal medium through which most people obtain visual entertainment and information and through which advertisers reach the largest audiences" (p. 3). Television performs two simultaneous functions, particularly in relation to gender: illustrating dominant ideals and teaching youth how to act (Tuchman, Daniels, and Benet, 1978). Early work on gender and television noted the symbolic annihilation of women, or lack of representation (Tuchman, 1978). Other scholars have noted that television reproduces contemporary dominant ideologies beyond gender (for example, Fiske, 1987; Hall, 1980/1991). Indeed, within television "the text delineates the terrain within which meanings may be made and proffers some meanings more vigorously than others" (Fiske, 1987, p. 16). This foremost set of meanings corresponds with dominant ideology. The dominant ideology in contemporary America supports the extant cultural, economic, and institutional status quo. Since its inception "television has always been a medium encoded with the meanings prevalent in the society to which it appeals" (Butler, 2006, p. 10). Thus, television illustrates the "dominant culture order," replete with class, gender, and race societal structures (Hall, 1980/1991).

While many consider television to reflect the dominant ideals of Western culture, Meehan (2005) avers that this notion is naïve and overly simplistic; rather, the depicted version of America is constructed by a conglomerate-controlled media system focused on finances and thus does not proffer an accurate representation of America or its culture. Instead, broadcasters appeal to the largest audience possible by airing bland and broadly understood content (Fiske, 1987). Larger audiences beget higher advertising rates. Meehan (2005) points out that even the niche cable channels, owned by gigantic media corporations, still strive for the biggest base of consumers. The myriad Kardashian series are broadcast on the specialized cable channel E!. E! is part of NBC Universal, which in turn is fifty-one percent owned by the Comcast Corporation. General Electric owns the remaining forty-nine percent (*Who Owns What*, 2012). While television may reflect the biases of its corporate owners, and is designed to earn revenue, conclusions may still be drawn about dominant social norms and behaviors, as television must resonate with audience's understanding of social order in order to attain viewers. Television programs thus necessarily embody and reflect American society. Moreover, reality TV is especially significant as it purports to depict true American lives, reflecting American hopes, desires, and dreams.

Keeping Up with the Kardashians and its spin-offs are considered to be reality television. Reality TV "circulates ideologies, myths, and templates for living" (Ouelette & Murray, 2009, p. 4) and has alternately been deemed a marketing designation (Friedman, 2002), a consequence of cost cutting (Raphael, 2009), an evolution of documentary production (Corner, 2002), or a symptom of American culture's descent into abasement (Juzwiak, 2011). This book follows Ouelette and Murray's definition: reality TV is "an unabashed commercial genre united less by aesthetic rules or certainties than by the fusion of popular entertainment with a self-conscious claim to the discourse of the real" (2009, p. 3). This definition takes into account both "the merger of marketing and 'real-life' entertainment [and] the convergence of new technologies with programs and their promotion" (Ouelette & Murray, 2009, p. 3). Accordingly, reality TV denotes the recent avalanche of programming that is ostensibly unscripted while also heavily commodified.

Ouelette and Murray (2009) also contend the democratic potential of reality TV, the supposed addition of a diverse range of people into the public sphere, has been co-opted by commercial aspects. The fiscal intentions of reality TV override the ancillary benefits. People are producing and participating in reality TV not to add an opinion to the democratic cacophony of voices, but instead to claim and capitalize upon their fifteen minutes of fame.

GENDER ON TV

In regard to gender, broadcast television hegemonically defines how women and men should behave professionally, sexually, and in relation to others, as well as teaches viewers how to understand gendered culture (e.g., Kellner, 1995; Tuchman, 1978; Wood, 2011). While these meanings may adapt over time, they are resilient (Dow, 2006). Depictions of gender on television support and occasionally challenge traditional norms and expectations of women. In general, television inculcates stereotypes and mediated definitions of womanhood and manhood.

Media "shapes our understanding of gender" (Wood, 2011, p. 257) by providing "models of what it means to be male or female" (Kellner, 1995, p. 1). Additionally, throughout varied media forms, advertising represents the supposed ultimate essence of gender (Jhally, 2006). While women and minorities are underrepresented on TV, "most media images reflect long-established cultural stereotypes of masculinity and femininity" (Wood, 2011, p. 272).

On television, white men are typically depicted as serious, competent, and powerful (Brooks & Hebert, 2006; Walsh & Ward, 2008). However, within the majority of reality television, while still powerful, men in general are stereotyped as immature or insensitive (Wood, 2011). As they embody conventional notions of masculinity, reality-TV men are "seldom shown nurturing others or doing housework" (Wood, 2011, p. 263). Moreover, on the many reality dating competitions, men evidence "manliness" by degrading women (Pozner, 2004).

Just as television stereotypes men and women, it also reinforces stereotypical male/female relationships. Men are portrayed as authoritative and independent, while women are illustrated as incompetent, reliant upon men, and primarily domestic (Wood, 2011). Typically, television portrayals feature women in the domestic sphere, caring for home and children, while men have worthwhile public-sphere careers (Brunsdon, D'Acci, & Spigel, 1997). Walsh and Ward (2008) assert that women are often depicted shopping, grooming, and engaging in domestic activities while male characters are shown working, building, fighting, and thinking. Reality TV especially validates the conceptions of men as stoic providers and women as compliant subjects in need of direction, relegated to the private sphere (Douglas, 2010; Pozner, 2010). Likewise, Holtzman (2000) avers that televised women are preoccupied with men, children, relationships, and housework. Furthermore, women and girls are frequently represented as submissive (Jhally & Katz, 2001; Walsh & Ward, 2008), while men are often depicted as aggressive and violent, with women as victims (Wood, 2011).

Relationships other than sexual are depicted as well. Television reiterates familial norms, such as an upper-middle class lifestyle and the notion of a nuclear family (Kompare, 2009). Kompare (2009) notes *The Osbournes*, featuring a mom, dad, sister, and brother, was the first of the modern day reality television series focused upon a family. The success of *The Osbournes* begets many offspring: *Snoop Dogg's Fatherhood, Jon and Kate Plus 8, 18 Kids and Counting, Gene Simmons Family Jewels, Run's House*, and *Keeping Up with the Kardashians*, among others. According to the Kardashian sisters themselves, "if we had to say who we were most like, it would be *The Osbournes*, because they were wacky, too; but they all loved each other a lot" (Kardashian et al., 2011, p. 108). Several of these programs test the parameters of familial norms; however, many feature a nuclear family, if a little unusual in behavior or makeup. Nearly all of the participants within programs of this ilk conform to standard gender norms.

Significantly, reality-dating programs are known for reducing participants to stereotypes. In particular *The Bachelor*, featuring a bevy of beauties competing for a single man, encourages a "game" for the audience of judging women solely on superficial attributes (Gray, 2009). Women participating on the program are often illustrated as scheming, manipulative, and sexually promiscuous. However, polysomic meanings may be gleaned from various dating shows, offering differing versions of femininity (Gray, 2009). Fiske (1989) contends that dating shows illustrate parity, in that both men and women are free to choose a mate, thus challenging patriarchal standards. However, the post-2000 crop of reality TV dating programs, primarily illustrated by enduringly popular paterfamilias *The Bachelor*, which has been airing since 2002, defies this contention. Gray (2009) avers "reality TV dating shows' structures appear to reward women for relishing the roles of sexual object and spectacle and the old duality of the Madonna and the whore" (p. 266).

Given this context of televised stereotypes and norms, as well as the Kardashian family's growing popularity, the portrayal of women and family as represented within *Keeping Up with the Kardashians* indicates an important element of popular culture to investigate.

KEEPING UP WITH THE KARDASHIANS

Throughout media, women are encouraged to be sexual and passive, corresponding to cultural feminine ideals, yet then objectified for these qualities (Jhally & Katz, 2001; Wood, 2011). Reality television is "particularly strong in reinforcing traditional views of women and what makes women desirable" (Wood, 2011, p. 265). The Kardashian women are far from passive, although correspond with sexual norms. Considering the prevalence of the media environment, the Kardashian family's growing popularity indicates an important element of popular culture to investigate, meriting thorough study. In total, over the course of the seven seasons several contradictory values (family/business, gender role contravention, intimacy/transgressions, narcissism/celebrity, beauty/unhappiness, sexual/conservative) were illustrated overtly and implicitly. Moreover, three particular themes were visible throughout the series: materialism, hard work, and perfect weddings, all pertaining to conspicuous consumption. This chapter discusses the first three dichotomies; the next examines the latter three, as well as the themes.

Family/Business

The most dominant conflation of contradictory values is the family/business pairing. In the first episode of the first season, Kris illustrates the family/business duality by clarifying her twinned role of mother and manager of her relatives' careers. Her role as a self-described "momager" blends family and business principles. When Kim is asked to appear on the Tyra Banks talk show, with the caveat of necessarily discussing a pornographic recording in which she appeared, Kris explained: "When I first heard about Kim's tape [sex tape], as her mother I wanted to kill her. But as her manager, I knew I had a job to do and I really just wanted her to move past it." Each role has dissonant expectations and beliefs. A mother might bemoan her daughter's behavior, scolding her judgment; a manager must exploit the situation to her client's benefit. The roles of businesswoman and mother are intermingled through actions, relationships, and settings.

In the first season, Kim discusses her mother's recent rash of mistakes in managing Kim's career (S1, E2). As a prank, Khloé (operating at Kim's behest to teach mom a lesson) tells her mother that Kim may be firing her as manager. Kris immediately overreacts, changing her outgoing answering machine message to inform callers of Kim's personal telephone number. By the end of this episode, in true television fashion, everyone realizes that family is paramount. Additionally, Kim learns a lesson about the amount of work her mother truly performs as her manager, signifying the value conflict between business and family. Kim assures her mom that not only does she love her, but she wants her to continue managing her career. The heart to heart conversation Kim and Kris have about her professional performance occurs while Khloé and Kourtney yell and roughhouse in the background, highlighting the physical merging of business and family.

In another representative example, when Khloé considers moving to New York, Kris's reaction is complicated by her dual role. Kris cries and protests; a possible good career move is negated by a mother's need to be close to her child.

Another factor that highlights the conflation of the business and mother roles is the location of many business discussions: the home. The home is traditionally a feminine and private sphere, free from public sphere commercial decisions. However, the Kardashians often evaluate business decisions at home. In season one, when Kris and Bruce, Kim's stepfather, discuss Kim posing for *Playboy*, this professional conversation is conducted in the kitchen of their house, while Kris bakes dessert.

Kris is much more frequently depicted in a business role, even within the home, than performing motherly duties. These duties, such as carpooling and buying school supplies, are delegated to stepfather Bruce. The role of mother is usurped by the managerial duties. The contradictory values of mother and manager coexist, with managerial characteristics dominating.

The relationships of all the family members are seemingly strengthened through working together and supporting each other's business endeavors. Whereas most people separate their two worlds of work and family, the Kardashians consistently intertwine the two areas. For example, when Kendall expresses her desire to model, her mother immediately begins to find Kendall modeling work (S2, E8). The episode ends with Kendall modeling for clothing retailer Forever 21, with all of her sisters attending the photoshoot, blurring the lines of work and family by their presence.

At the start of the series, Kris manages only Kim and Bruce; by the end of season seven, she manages all six of her children, working with other people in her employ. The gradual process of Kris's acquisition of clients is exemplified by Kourtney's decision to hire her, in the second episode of season three. Kourtney evaluates the conflicting roles her mother fulfills and her efficacy as manager, finally deciding her mother truly executes her managerial role well.

Kourtney complicates the issue by considering if her mother will favor Kim's career over Kourtney's. Sibling rivalry, in this case, carries over into the professional world, as a mother's preference can not only hurt feelings, but earnings as well. Indeed, while Kris successfully negotiates Kourtney's cover appearance for *944* magazine, she then opts to attend a publicity event with Kim over Kourtney's first solo photo-shoot. After Kourtney seethes over her mother's decision, Kris redeems herself by obtaining Kourtney a well-paid spread in *Maxim* magazine. Kourtney accepts her mother's apology, and the audience is treated to images of Kourtney at the *Maxim* shoot, being photographed in skimpy lingerie.

Later in season three, during episode five, at the sisters' Dash clothing store, Kris happily shares with Kourtney and Khloé that she has just procured Kim a perfume deal for a fragrance named Dashing. Kris and Kim had trademarked that name for fragrances two years earlier in anticipation of releasing a perfume. Kourtney and Khloé react angrily; mad for a variety of reasons, they claim to primarily be infuriated for the exclusion by their manager/mom and sister. At lunch they discuss the business of the perfume in the context of their familial emotions: Kris avers that Kim's fragrance builds the Kardashian brand, benefitting the entire family. Kourtney and Khloé's sisterly envy initially prevents them from recognizing this.

Kris' role as manager conflicts with her role of peacekeeping, equitable mother. The fragrance naming issue is resolved when Kris begins to cry during another discussion of the dilemma. Kourtney then cries as well, and the mother and sisters reconcile. Although not mentioned on the program, an outcome of this issue is that Kim's first fragrance is eponymous. Kim and Kris concede the name of the fragrance in exchange for familial support of the Kardashian brand, as well as family peace. The Kardashian brand rests upon solidarity; familial acrimony potentially harms the family's commercial interests.

That Kris is the manager is never forgotten; it appears frequently on the program. When Khloé rhetorically asks why a photograph of Kim is her mother's screensaver, Kourtney answers by citing the typical managerial agreement: mom gets ten percent (S1, E8). Kim is the perceived favorite because of her earning potential for the family. These off-handed comments are woven into dialogue throughout the series.

The dichotomy of family and business is played out not only through Kris and her momager role but also exemplified by Kim's struggle to balance the two. This duality is illustrated as Kim attempts to maintain a successful long-distance relationship with Reggie Bush, a professional football player based in New Orleans, and sustain her career (S3, E8). In a voiceover, Kim describes her hectic, work-filled life of photo-shoots for magazines and calendars, running her co-owned shoe company Shoedazzle, and shooting film and TV roles. Her voiceover runs over a montage of flashbulbs erupting, photo-shoots, photos of her posing, framed photos of her, ads for Shoedazzle, hugging Robert Shapiro from Shoedazzle, and posing with fans. Her time-consuming career hampers her relationship with Reggie Bush.

Reggie requests that Kim attend his season-opener game in New Orleans; however, Kim has a conflicting personal appearance. Kris, acting in her motherly role of advice-giver, explains Kim needs to be there for the game and for Reggie. Kim opts to attend the game, watching from a private box with family and friends, even though she has doubts about missing her event.

She reconsiders at the game, impressed with Reggie's popularity after noticing the numerous fans wearing his endorsed jersey. By the end of the episode, Kim has come to the realization that Reggie makes her happy. Viewed with the knowledge that Kim and Reggie's relationship ultimately didn't work, audience members are left to wonder if Kim was truly in love with him, or merely wowed by Reggie's celebrity, or chose her career over him. Regardless, the relationship difficulties emphasize how hard it is for Kim to maintain a personal life, due to the intertwining of her business and private life. After all, every component of her life is fodder for the reality show and press coverage. Kim's personal life is public.

By the second episode of season four, Reggie and Kim have broken up, and her poor mood is apparently affecting her work. As Kim seemingly rebounds from the break up at the end of the episode, she again frames her personal life in terms of her career, deciding that not only does she need to focus on her business life, but Reggie does as well. Kim's romantic life is only discussed in terms of how it affects and is affected by her work, enhancing the Kardashian conflation of personal and business realms. The episode ends with a successful photo shoot for the advertising campaign of Kim's new fragrance.

The series recurrently depicts Kim "working." In season four's tenth episode—also notable for exemplifying Kourtney's boyfriend Scott's terrible behavior—Kim makes a personal appearance at a Las Vegas nightclub for her birthday, commodifying another aspect of her life. Kris warns her of the promotional requirements and suggests she might want to take her birthday off. Kris explains Kim's required activities, including various appearances and a fan meeting, each of which she must stay a requisite number of hours. As Kris speaks, another montage plays, featuring photo shoots, Shoedazzle promotions, planes landing and taking off, paparazzi, fashion shows, and finally, Kim signing autographs. Moreover, Kris worries about a commercial shoot for the West Coast fast food chain, Carl's Jr., scheduled to film the day after Kim's birthday. Kim appears compulsively driven to work, albeit the "work of being watched" or being herself for the camera and audience (Andrejevic, 2004).

The day of Kim's birthday, Kris has a meeting scheduled to take place in Las Vegas with Keith Frankel, an executive at QuickTrim, the weight-loss nutritional supplement company with which the family works. Scott has been working for QuickTrim securing promotional endorsements, a job that Kris obtained for him. Blackout drunk, Scott embarrasses himself at dinner in front of his employers. Despite the ensuing family quarrel, Kim successfully fulfills her appearance requirements and attends the photo shoot the next day. The episode ends with Kim realizing her mother is right; Kim should take some time off to balance out her time-consuming work commitments. In this rare event, Kris's mother role triumphs over the managerial function.

The tension between family and business depicted on the program may resonate with audiences; many working families struggle to balance the two. Additionally, whereas Walsh and Ward (2008) found women on television were most often depicted in domestic activities, by contrast the Kardashians are frequently shown in work-related pursuits, as is common for off-screen families. While the Kardashians' version of the family/business dichotomy is over-the-top—as illustrated through arguments and tears, as is their wont—this relatable issue may draw fans. Furthermore, their struggle to balance personal and business lives is glamorous; Kim must choose between photo-shoots and an NFL player boyfriend. Kardashian lives are messy, yet not mundane, understated, or boring.

More often than not, the Kardashians choose work over play, and then incorporate family into the work. This blending of family and work is unrealistic for most Americans, yet may signal a foregone ideal, the family laboring together for the betterment of the whole, akin to a family farm or a family store. Concurrently, the ideal of family spending time together while working masks the true nature of their "work"; the promotion of themselves and Kardashian-related products, as exemplified through the entire concept of the reality program. Viewers see the Kardashians "working" by posing for photographers and attending events, yet in truth, they are consistently working the entire time while being recorded for the program, performing the "work of being watched" (Andrejevic, 2004). As reality television participants, their entire recorded lives is work. Family-focused reality television may be the new version of the family farm; all members toiling together to benefit the overall unit.

Gender Role Contravention

With Kris represented as the income-generating manager, Bruce takes on the traditionally female role of caregiver. Bruce completes errands, looks after the two youngest daughters, and generally runs the household. While ostensibly appreciated, like many off-screen women, his voice is often unheeded or unheard on the program.

Not only does Bruce represent the established wifely role, he is also the voice of conservative values. Along with his motherly duties of providing general care for the youngest children, he is also the enforcer of traditional values. When eleven-year-old Kylie is ready to go to school sporting red lipstick and heavy eye makeup, he forces her to remove it before driving her and her sister to school (S3, E 11). Kris and Bruce argue over Kylie's cosmetic use, but ultimately Bruce explains this is his arena of dominion, forbidding makeup and boys. The space Bruce refers to may be construed as the private sphere, while Kris literally governs the family's public sphere in her managerial role, determining in which media outlets the family will appear.

Later, Bruce, Kris, Khloé, Kendall, and Kylie eat dinner in a restaurant. Kylie is wearing makeup again and dressed in a cleavage-baring outfit. Bruce is upset: Kylie has learned how to trigger her father's anger by mimicking her sisters' traits. After a loud argument, Bruce and Kylie leave dinner early as other diners turn around and stare. Bruce and Kris disagree about parenting, and compromise by modifying Kylie's grounding punishment. After discussing the issue with her father, Kylie promises not to grow up too fast. The plotline resolves and old home footage of Kylie as a little girl plays.

The family is often afraid of Bruce's moralistic disapproval. On the first season, Girls Gone Wild founder Joe Francis calls from prison, requesting that the Kardashians become spokes models for his high-end bikini line (S1, E3). He offers to fly them to his beachfront mansion in Puerto Vallarta, Mexico for a photo shoot, to which they readily agree. When asked if she's told Bruce about the photo shoot, Kris demurs by citing Bruce's conservative values, and claiming to not want to upset him.

This recurs again and again; when the family assumes Bruce won't approve of a decision, they try not to tell him about it until the last possible moment, resulting in drama-filled scenes. Bruce is the voice of prudence, which often results in the family laughing at him and his disgust with them. The roles of the typical patriarchal family are reversed; Bruce is ignored, while the women in the family dictate the norms by which the family abides. This is another example of how *Keeping Up with the Kardashians* challenges the standard reality TV conventions of white men being depicted as powerful and dominant (Brooks & Hebert, 2006) and women as reliant upon men (Wood, 2011). Here, the Kardashian domestic norms upend traditional television standards.

Upon finding out about the bikini shoot, Bruce flies to Mexico, confronting his wife about lying to him. Kris is embarrassed that he's there, not sad or regretful that she lied by omission. Ultimately, while Bruce can express his unhappiness and dismay, he has no agency. He often states his dissenting opinion, which the family then scorns. The family ostensibly is afraid to tell him things and incur his wrath; why is unclear, as they simply disregard him anyway. When Kim elects to pose for *Playboy*, Bruce is against it, noting that a *Playboy* spread in conjunction with Kim's sex tape could negatively affect her image. In this family, father may know best, but no one pays him any attention.

In Kris's role as manager, she controls the family assets, including the household finances; circumventing another means Bruce could exert any power. In season four, episode five, Bruce asks Kris for his own bank account, saying that he dislikes having to ask her for coffee money. She flippantly refuses, noting he has a Starbucks card.

If the names were reversed, this exchange would seem more likely to occur in 1950 rather than 2010. In his personal narrative to the camera, Bruce laments Kris's controlling nature. However, Bruce's reason for desiring direction over his finances is trivial; he would like to add to his collection of miniature helicopters, which Kris considers a waste of money. However, while denying Bruce the ability to buy luxuries she profligately spends on clothing, purchasing a $4,000 dress for an event.

Bruce asks Khloé to borrow money, explaining Kris controls the books; he doesn't have a personal checking account or credit cards. Although Kris may be unduly authoritative, Khloé undermines her mother by endeavoring to give Bruce money. Khloé scornfully dubs Bruce a little girl and a puss, and in coarse terms, notes Kris's dominance over Bruce. Khloé's derogatory use of feminine terms demean women. While helping Bruce, Khloé forces him to renounce his masculine gender, to actually verbalize in vulgar terms that he holds the role of the ineffectual, powerless wife, unable to make any decisions without permission.

Khloé also belittles Bruce for having to appeal to her, asserting her dominance over him. By lending Bruce the money, she contends she wants him to "feel like a man," which connotes a variety of gender norms and expectations, including that of men being more powerful than women.

The gender role contravention also plays out through another couple featured on the series: Kourtney and Scott. Scott voices the stereotypical gender expectations, while Kourtney exemplifies the Kardashian matriarchy.

In an example, Scott refuses to attend a breastfeeding class with Kourtney; to him, breastfeeding is clearly her job. He explicitly refers to gender as to why he is not required to attend. Instead, Khloé attends the class with Kourtney, noting that she's "the dad."

Eventually, Kourtney tires of Scott's attitude, and gives him an ultimatum: help with the impending baby or the relationship is over. In response, Scott assembles a crib, apparently acquiescing to Kourtney's not unreasonable demands.

Kim and Kris Humphries's doomed relationship also illustrates the Kardashian gender culture in which women make the decisions, men are typically ignored, and stereotypical behaviors are noted and then transgressed. Kris notices the female-dominated Kardashian value system, which Khloé affirms by saying "in this family . . . men have no say so what-so-ever" (S6, E14).

Later, speaking to Kim, Humphries says, "I just don't want to end up like Scott and Bruce, like not having any say. Just basically living life in the passenger seat. Not even, in the back seat" (S6, E14).

In another conversation representative of the shows depiction of male and female stereotypes, Humphries questions Rob's habit of receiving weekly manicures/pedicures, slighting Rob's masculinity. However, in typical Kardashian fashion of stating gender roles and then challenging them, Humphries then permits Kim to give him a pedicure, indulging in a stereotypically feminine grooming habit. They often recognize gender roles and then challenge expectations.

However, Humphries provides a benchmark of stereotypical roles in his expectations. In an example, he places a pet dog on the kitchen counter. Kim reacts in disgust, while Humphries argues, "You don't cook anyway. You don't cook!"

The Kardashians both support and subvert gender stereotypes. They comply with Kompare's (2009) assertion that television reinforces prevailing concepts of an upper-middle class lifestyle and nuclear family familial norms. However, they disrupt other accepted gender-related contentions. As noted previously, on television men are primarily depicted as competent and dominant (Brooks & Hebert, 2006; Walsh & Ward, 2008), while women are frequently illustrated as passive (Jhally & Katz, 2001; Walsh & Ward, 2008). Pozner (2010) argues reality TV specifically positions men as providers and women as acquiescent subjects. The Kardashians contravene typical television conventions by giving Bruce no agency and forcing Scott to adapt. Additionally, a reason for Kris Humphries and Kim's divorce could be Humphries' lack of deference to the Kardashian women-dominated system of governance. Moreover, the family is a matriarchy in which women rule not only the roost, but the family's public sphere as well, which violates the television norm of men being featured within the public domain and women within the domestic area (Brunsdon, D'Acci, & Spigel, 1997).

Intimacy/Transgressions

Throughout the series, the intimacy of the family is illustrated repetitively. However, their closeness is transgressive, too close, breaking traditional taboos and standards, particularly those related to sex. This is undoubtedly related to the daughters' sexual images, necessarily discussed with their dual mother/manager. The lack of parent/children boundaries is part of the show's appeal, as audience members may watch to see which taboos will be broken.

A first season episode titled "Remembering Dad" demonstrates their closeness. It focuses on the family's commemoration of Robert Kardashian, Sr., the patriarch of the Kardashian family. In particular, Khloé has difficulties with her anger and sadness related to his death. Through editing and dialogue, this program associates his death with Khloé being arrested for drunk driving. The family joins together to eulogize their father and help Khloé with her issues. In this episode, Khloé must contend with two judgmental fathers. Kris provokes Khloé, asking her to consider what the deceased Robert Kardashian, Sr. would think; Khloé must also face her stepfather Bruce's disapproval of her arrest. The episode ends with a montage of home movies of Robert Kardashian, Sr. The Kardashians' collective grief over this loss bonds the individual family members into a cohesive unit.

Robert Kardashian, Sr.'s absence is mentioned regularly on the show. Through discourse, the family mythologizes him into a superlative father, equally loving and knowledgeable, proffering advice and guidance. Robert Kardashian, Jr. memorializes his father by tattooing his face on his forearm, a large image of which his mother disapproves (S3, E6). Kim intuitively reasons that as Rob graduates from his father's alma mater, he misses his dad.

While the family members often converse about how much they miss their father, Rob also discusses about his lack of a father figure growing up. This upsets Bruce, who served as a surrogate father throughout Rob's childhood. They began living in the same home upon Kris and Bruce's marriage in 1991, when Rob was four, Khloé seven, Kim eleven, and Kourtney twelve (although Kourtney lived with Robert Kardashian, Sr. after the divorce). Bruce is continually forgotten in the shadow of the deceased patriarch, never able to live up to the vaunted memory of Robert Kardashian, Senior. Accordingly, when Khloé marries, she selects Rob to walk her down the aisle, instead of Bruce, despite his father-figure role. Only upon Rob's demur and other family members' coaxing does she permit Bruce to symbolically give her away. Even Kris, who cheated on and then divorced Robert Kardashian, proclaims to miss his wisdom and guidance, sobbing her grief and visiting his grave (S3, E1). Kris repeatedly claims to regret her actions and the end of their marriage. The absence of Robert Kardashian also draws the family closer, helping to heal the rift evident from Kris and Robert's acrimonious split. The family members bond over what they construe as an immense loss, continually and freshly feeling the bereavement upon every new event in their lives, bonding them tightly together.

Yet their intimate relationships infringe on typical familial limitations. While the family is tightly knit, they are too close, potentially jarring viewers out of their comfort zone. Historically, family dramas rarely feature the taboo-crossing situations the Kardashians devise.

In an example illustrative of the boundary-breaking nature of their close-knit relationships, Kim's anniversary gift for Bruce and Kris is a stripper pole (S1, E1). This gift shatters American parent/child relationship and familial sexuality norms. Later, twelve-year-old Kylie finds Kim showing the gift to anniversary party guest Robyn Anton, founder of the female burlesque/pop group Pussycat Dolls. Kim and Robyn watch in surprise as the pre-teen sexily dances and slides up and down the pole. The hi-jinks end when Bruce strolls into the room, reprimands Kim, and carries a yelling Kylie out of the room. The stripper pole maybe a funny gag gift for parents, albeit a risqué one, but it also shows the family's nonchalance about sexuality and sex. While Bruce, the conservative voice of reason, deems that the stripper pole is an inappropriate plaything for Kylie, it still exists in their house, representative of the high-level of sexual talk prevalent in their household. This demeaning of the significance of sex has visible results in oldest sister Kourtney's supposedly unplanned pregnancy. Of course, the lack of parent/children boundaries may be part of the show's appeal: which taboos will they break next?

Other examples abound throughout the initial episode, setting the tone for the rest of the series. At Kris and Bruce's anniversary party, pre-teens Kendall and Kylie play at bartending, mixing drinks and dancing behind the bar. Later, Khloé's toast to her stepfather includes a vasectomy joke, as everyone watching laughs (S1, E1).

The family seemingly has no restrictions on behavior. Kris breaches the normal demarcation lines between family and nonfamily members as she intrudes on her daughter Kourtney's relationship. Kris apparently has no inhibitions telling Kourtney's boyfriend that he is too young for her, not ready to settle down, and intimates that he cheats on her (E1, S1). Later, Khloé explains to her mother that she should stay out of her family's personal lives but Kris disagrees, noting privacy is not a Kardashian value.

Indeed, the family often encroaches upon each other's relationships. Over the course of the series, they repeatedly involve themselves in Kourtney and Scott's tumultuous relationship, as well as in Rob's relationships with various women. Later in season one, during Kourtney and Scott's pregnancy scare in the episode titled "You are so pregnant dude," Khloé refers to her sister and her boyfriend as bitches, and declares they should use condoms in the future. Seemingly not learning from this episode, Kourtney later refers to her season four pregnancy as welcome, yet accidental.

In another example, the sisters ignore how Rob prefers his family to interact with girlfriend Adrienne. Likewise, Kim and Kourtney sign Khloé up for an online dating service, creating a profile and arranging blind dates without her knowledge (S2, E5). As Kim once said, "When you date one of us, you kind of date the whole family" (S4, E1).

In addition to inappropriate behavior, their language is often coarse; sexual talk is a constant on the show. For example, on the fourth episode of season two, Kourtney and Khloé search for their mother's vibrator, although she and Bruce protest its existence. After the fruitless search, Khloé asks where they keep their dildo. In the same episode, the older sisters take it upon themselves to teach their two younger sisters about menses, complete with a demonstration involving water and a tampon. The episode ends with the family watching the video of Kris giving birth to Kendall.

The examples of sexual language are myriad and are usually spoken by Khloé. She often engages in crude talk to provoke laughs, instigate fights, or direct attention away from herself. For example, when conversation turns to her drunk driving arrest, she derails the discussion, changing the conversation to be about her mother and Bruce having sex (S3, E1).

The most glaring example of Khloé's vulgar conduct occurs on a family camping trip undertaken by the Kardashians and Rob's girlfriend Adrienne's family (S3, E10). In an effort to provoke laughs and perhaps scare the outsiders, Khloé repeatedly utters obscene comments. Rob expects this to occur, noting that his sisters like to embarrass him. To this end, Khloé instigates a question/answer game for the families to play. If the person being questioned refuses to answer, he or she must drink a shot of tequila. Khloé asks her mother to choose between two sexual acts with Bruce; Kourtney follows by asking Rob to choose which of two sexual embarrassing stories about him she should relate. Lastly, Khloé asks Adrienne, Rob's girlfriend, to choose between two sexual acts with Rob. At this purposely-offensive question, Adrienne's father walks away, escaping the pastime. No one does anything to stop the game.

Afterward, Rob asks Kim to tell Khloé and Kourtney to stop making sexual comments. Typically, Rob is powerless when facing the women in his matriarchal family, his desires and opinions pushed aside. His request for Kim to intercede indicates recognition of lack of agency. Kim agrees that no one listens to Rob, blaming birth order for his impotency, but also noting that he should "just grow up and be a man and stand up for himself." Overcoming his fear, Rob tells his family to respect their guests and behave. The family knows when they are crossing the line of polite comportment and chooses to step over it, reveling in their outrageous behavior. Presumably, these shocking elements of the show draw viewers as well.

The sexual nature is not limited to talk. In an episode memorable for its comedic, sitcom-like plot, Kris surreptitiously drugs Bruce's coffee with an organic male enhancement pill (S4, E3). After a few sex-filled days, in which the audience sees the couple make out in the kitchen and repair to their bedroom, to the chagrin of their kids, Rob accidentally drinks Bruce's coffee and must visit the emergency room as a result. This episode is notable for breaking the invisible taboo of middle-aged people being sexual on television. Typically, televised sexuality is reserved for only young and stereotypically beautiful people; people over fifty are very rarely sexualized.

Later on in season four, another plotline concerns sex; namely, the lack of it being indulged in by eight-months-pregnant Kourtney and her boyfriend Scott (S4, E9). The story arc begins with the two of them in bed as Scott demands sex. Scott redeems his crassness later in the episode by expressing a sweeter thought; sex is more than physical fulfillment, but engenders intimacy. Kourtney claims that she's afraid intercourse will hurt the baby. In order to rectify this situation, they attend a sex class for pregnant couples. Before they attend the class, Kris overshares her experiences with pregnancy and sex, declaring that being pregnant increased her sex drive, while her daughters groan in embarrassment. At the class, Kourtney and Scott, as well as the other couples attending, learn different positions, as depicted in a montage of the two of them in varied sexual positions, as well as talking about connecting emotionally. The story arc resolves with Scott and Kourtney in their bedroom, candles lit and rose petals scattered, and Scott closing the door on the camera.

Another element of the series that may be considered distasteful and unusual for a family program is the graphic depiction of medical procedures. When Bruce needs a colonoscopy, he explains it in detail, including the requirement to evacuate his bowels prior to the procedure. Viewers see a humorous montage of Bruce heading into the bathroom repeatedly (S3, E4). This sequence ends with footage from inside Bruce's colon, shot during the colonoscopy. This season also includes Khloé having a mole removed and close-up shots of Kim's eyeballs as she receives LASIK surgery. The video of Kim's LASIK surgery is embedded on the Maloney Vision Institute's website, suggesting that she received some form of compensation in return for televising the procedure.

Other medical procedures include the family's myriad plastic surgeries, Scott's visit to a doctor to inquire about a vasectomy (S7, E17), and Khloé and Kim's visit to a fertility clinic (S7, E17). At the fertility clinic, both Khloé and Kim undergo ultrasounds and other tests; Kim's results are normal, while Khloé learns she has not ovulated that month. In the next episode, the conclusion of the two-part season finale, the doctor prescribes Khloé drugs (oral and injected) to encourage ovulation, Kim contemplates freezing her eggs, and Kourtney gives birth (S7, E18).

In fact, the most graphic medical procedures depicted on the show are the births of Kourtney's two children (S4, E11; S7, E18). Scott, not a professional cameraman, shot the footage of the first birth. Kourtney explains that she did not want a camera crew in the delivery room, yet later decided to share the amateur recording. During the first intensely graphic scene of birth, Kourtney is calm while everyone else cries (almost the entire family is in the delivery room). During the baby's birth, Kourtney reaches down, grabs him, and pulls him the rest of the way out, which she does with her daughter as well. Their son's name is Mason Dash Disick. Dash is also the name of the clothing store Kourtney, Kim, and Khloé own. While graphic births are depicted on other reality shows, namely TLC's *A Baby Story* and *Birth Day*, it is unusual for a program not explicitly about birth or medicine to graphically present labor and childbirth. These births reify the closeness of the Kardashian clan, illustrating how they all gather together for momentous occasions, and transparently exhibiting their emotions. Moreover, these televised celebrity births connote tacit approval of the contemporary way of giving birth: in a hospital, provided pharmaceutical intervention, with the mother strapped to the table and barely able to move. Furthermore, in season four Kourtney pauses to shave before going to the hospital and wears a full face of make-up, retaining her beautiful and glamorous image even while undergoing an exhausting, painful ordeal. Her televised composure and familial gathering exemplify the dichotomy of the Kardashian intimacy; a tightly-bonded family, willing to expose their most intimate moments, potentially engendering disgust, fascination, and envy toward their bonds and indecencies.

CONCLUSION

The family illustrates the complexities of simultaneously attempting to maintain traditional morals while endorsing newer, modern ethics. Bruce voices many conservative morals, as documented, which the family chooses to ignore. However, the family endeavors to ensure quality time together sans outside distractions, like phones (although reality television crews are apparently okay). The family also exemplifies current liberal values, never once remarking upon the family members' many interracial romantic relationships and accepting various homosexual friends. All forms of sexuality are, in fact, celebrated on the show, which—while in opposition to conservative voices dominant in American politics—jibes with the sexual nature of contemporary media, visible in the rise of pay-cable networks and their dependence upon nudity, as well as the best-selling popularity of salacious books like *Fifty Shades of Grey*.

Another duality present throughout the series is the public/private sphere dichotomy and the role women fulfill in the home. Kris initially runs her management business from her home, merging the public and private spheres. These two fusions (business and family, public and private) result in a unique value system for the Kardashians. What other families may regard as off-limits, such as sexuality and public nudity—integral components of Kim and her sisters' images—is very much a part of their televised home life. Moreover, *Keeping Up with the Kardashians* subverts traditional gender roles. Kris is most frequently framed in a business light, illustrating her fruitful techniques of managing her family's careers. While televised women stereotypically care for children and run households (Brunsdon, D'Acci, & Spigel, 1997), Kris has seemingly delegated these duties to her husband. Kris and Bruce's business and personal relationships also challenge reality TV's usual norm of women as acquiescent to male partners (Pozner, 2010).

Within reality TV as a genre, women are frequently depicted negatively (Wood, 2011). In this sense, *Keeping Up with the Kardashians* bucks this trend, providing a role model for entrepreneurial women. Not only is Kris an entrepreneur, but her daughters are as well. Many of the shows' scenes take place in Dash, the sisters' co-owned clothing store. The women within the show disprove the stereotype that sexy women are not smart.

The Kardashians blur boundaries that are distinct in typical households. There are no clear demarcations in any of the dichotomies discussed here. The syntheses of family and business, permissible and objectionable sexual behavior, and traditional male and female gender roles result in a complex web of right and wrong. In *Keeping Up with the Kardashians* the only ideal clearly elucidated is a reliable and clichéd sitcom moral, the importance of family.

Chapter Three

Celebrity, Beauty, and Sexuality

Keeping Up with the Kardashians establishes and sustains the celebrity status of the Kardashians. It is particularly evident through the dualities of narcissism/celebrity, beauty/unhappiness, and sexual/conservative found within the series. Moreover, celebrity is inherently linked to beauty standards and the capitalistic economy. Celebrity hegemonically functions to maintain the American version of capitalism (Marshall, 1997; Rojek, 2001). Here, I review literature pertaining to celebrity, chiefly as concerns reality TV, and then analyze correlated aspects of *Keeping Up with the Kardashians*. Next, relevant themes present within the program are considered through a conspicuous consumption theoretical framework.

CELEBRITY

Today, the power of celebrity is undeniable and inescapable. Our modern world is permeated by fame; it is a marker of contemporary life (Redmond, 2006). Many scholars differentiate between various media-produced celebrities: literary (Moran, 2000), athletic (Giles, 2000), film (Dyer, 1986/2004; Ellis, 1992), television (Marshall, 1997), and music (Marshall, 1997). Celebrity may be considered either warranted by talent or constructed by media (Gamson, 1994). Celebrity, while perhaps stronger economically and more culturally relevant today than ever before, nevertheless has a clear ancestral lineage. Several excellent historical perspectives of celebrity exist—for example, Braudy (1997), De Cordova (1990), and Dyer (1986/2004). The literature reviewed here focuses on the intersection of celebrity, women, reality TV, and social media, as these are the most pertinent issues of interest for this study.

Two books first published in 1961 decried the emergence of the modern celebrity; celebrity based not on heroism or intrinsic greatness, but rather fame itself. Boorstin, in his pivotal work *The Image*, claimed the modern notion of celebrity is "the perfect embodiment of tautology: the most familiar is the most familiar" (p. 61). Lowenthal, in his book *Literature, Popular Culture, and Society*, agreed with Boorstin, and also connected celebrities, or "idols of consumption," with the increase in leisure time and the need to buy products to fill it. Correspondingly, a primary mode of examining celebrity production and upkeep considers it as a product (Turner, 2004). In this manner of analysis, celebrity is considered the result of celebrity industry machinations, including the design of profit. Thus, the celebrity's individual personality characteristics are generally unimportant; the end result, celebrity earning revenue, is the same no matter who occupies the celebrity position.

What is Celebrity?

According to Turner (2004, p. 9) celebrity may be considered in three differentiated ways: as "a genre of representation and a discursive effect; . . . a cultural formation that has a social function; . . . a commodity traded by the promotions, publicity, and media industries that produce these representations and their effects." These three ways of defining celebrity are clarified and then used throughout the Kardashian analysis.

Celebrity as a Discursive Effect

In this paradigm, celebrity is constructed and perpetuated through discourse (Turner, 2004). The celebrity is not contingent upon talent or heroism; rather, media manufactures fame. Accordingly, anyone may achieve fame, as illustrated by the examples of Paris Hilton and Kim Kardashian, as well as the multitudes of their reality TV brethren. Furthermore, once media discourse about a person ceases, fame decreases in tandem.

Currid-Halkett, affirming Boorstin, contends that "fame is pure renown—literally the sum of all the people who have heard a person's name and can connect it meaningfully with something else—a face, a brand, a voice, or an idea" (2010, p. 29). Celebrity as a discursive effect is "a social phenomenon that exists everywhere" (Currid-Halkett, 2010, p. 67). Hence, celebrity may be defined as the phenomenon of society collectively caring about certain people for reasons that far outweigh (or have nothing to do with) their talent or deserved fame. Moreover, being a part of social dialogue "generates millions of dollars in revenue for celebrities themselves and the various people and companies that latch onto these individuals" (Currid-Halkett, 2010, p. 6).

Without a media presence, a person cannot be construed as famous. Celebrity appears throughout all forms of media, ranging from seminal newspapers to tabloids to blogs. The "fusion of technology, free information, and our need to socially bond" creates an insatiable desire for information—celebrities help to fill this void (Currid-Halkett, 2010, p. 20). Media access and availability is an essential element of contemporary celebrity; "media—from print to television to blogs and online paparazzi sites—give us up to the minute visuals and news snippets on every star we could ever want to hear about while symbiotically giving those stars a channel to be heard" (Currid-Halkett, 2010, p. 14).

Why are people fascinated by celebrities, desiring to learn more information and thus consuming magazines, websites, and social media? According to Bonnie Fuller, former Editor-in-Chief of *Us Weekly* and *Star* magazines, "it's because we start to relate to them like they're our friends. I think we look up to them and look down on them and occasionally judge them, but at the end of the day we feel we know them" (Piazza, 2011, p. 10).

This is partly due to changing nature of media enabling the democratic leveling of celebrity attainment process. As Currid-Halkett noted, "the rise of reality TV shows (and their great popularity) and the use of social media to perpetuate all forms of celebrity have reduced barriers to entry unlike at any other point in history" (2010, pp. 194-5). The many reality programs featuring an audience vote exemplify democratic fame; we decide which contestant will make the best celebrity, in mimicry of the democratic political voting process. However, while fame may be democratic in that anyone may attain it, celebrity truly hegemonically functions to maintain the extant economic and cultural systems, producing stars and audiences (Marshall, 1997).

People appearing on reality TV do not need to adhere to the typical foundations of celebrity: beauty, wealth, talent, and/or class privilege. Instead, "democratic celebrity relies on our empathy or sympathy with the stars as individuals" (Currid-Halkett, 2010, p. 199). The audience members are interchangeable with the stars; they represent what we can attain (Dyer, 1986/2004). This "intimate fame" offers audiences a "real" relationship built on seemingly one-on-one interaction; "as 'real' as anything can be." Thus, para-social relationships "offer people transgressive models of identity" (Redmond, 2006, p. 38).

Reality TV Discourse

Reality TV may be defined as shows that feature "real people playing themselves" (Hall, 2009, p. 516). Audiences may be aware of the contrived nature of the shows, but studies have shown that this is irrelevant; instead, audiences desire authenticity, or veracity of emotions from participants (Hall, 2009; Hill, 2005).

Watts (2008) asserted that "reality celebrities are a unique contemporary phenomenon—people who are famous for performing a version of themselves on television" (p. 236). This fame is earned not solely through media hype but also "through the mediated myth of their essential selves" (Watts, 2008, p. 237). Therefore, "reality-TV stardom is thus a unique type of celebrity, based on an inherent contradiction—a public self-based on a highly mediated, constructed, and/or performed 'real' selfhood" (Watts, 2008, p. 239). Reality TV conflates the Goffman (1959) duality of the private and public selves; the private self is performed. Consequently, reality TV celebrities seemingly have no private persona: "reality-celebrities must continually act *as if* they are off camera" (Curnutt, 2009, p. 251).

The private persona is celebrated on television, thus becoming public. Whether or not this televised persona is authentic or not, audiences consume programs in search of authenticity (Hill, 2005; Holmes, 2004). Televised emotions validate authenticity (McClain, 2011).

Within reality television, the camera gaze and subsequent fame, "constitute and validate everyday reality (Turner, 2004, p. 62). The televised image substantiates self-constructed identity and dictates what normality should look like (Turner, 2004).

Celebrity as Social Function

A second means of interpreting celebrity is as a cultural formation with social functions (Hermes, 1995; Turner, 2004; Turner, Bonner, and Marshall, 2000). In this model, celebrity may be considered a "social process through which relationships, identity, and social and cultural norms are debated, evaluated, modified, and shared" (Turner, 2004, p. 24). Celebrities function semiotically, retaining meanings that are interpreted polysemically by audiences (Dyer, 1986/2004). Infrequently, celebrity may subvert dominant ideology through intertexual references. For example, Britney Spears' perfume, *Curious*, promotes sexual freedom (Redmond, 2006). Typically, however, celebrities embody dominant cultural meanings, informing audiences of norms and standards (Marshall, 1997; Rojek, 2001).

Talking and gossiping about celebrities has become an integral part of how "media texts come to have meaning" (Hermes, 1999, p. 71). Celebrities function as a family member would, informing and providing social currency, yet without the associated responsibilities of being a family member, enriching personal community (Turner, 2004). Through celebrities, people may discuss and evaluate melodramatic topics, such as death, divorce, and scandal (Turner, 2004). Celebrity may also provide a pleasurable escape from mundanity of daily life (Stacy, 1994).

Through media, celebrities are places of cultural meaning negotiation and organization (Marshall, 1997). As Dyer (1986/2004) noted "stars represent typical ways of behaving, feeling, and thinking in contemporary society, ways that have been socially, culturally, historically constructed" (p. 17).

Celebrities tell us what to wear, how to smell, how to lose weight, what to listen to, what movies to watch, and how to vote (Piazza, 2011, p. 18). Thus, analysis of celebrities permits examination of the norms and meanings present within culture.

Celebrity is also a means of defining individual identity (Turner, 2004). As celebrities play an increasingly larger role in global media content, it is understandable that celebrity frequently is "a primary location where the news and entertainment media participate in the construction of cultural identity" (Turner, 2004, p. 102). However, identity construction is a "highly contingent and negotiated social practice" (Turner, 2004, p. 103). Nonetheless, celebrities doubtlessly influence portions of identity construction in their audiences. Often audience members look to celebrities as a means of aiding in identity creation. This identity-building process links individual identity to celebrity and consumerism, a key facet of capitalism. Marshall (1997) notes celebrity discursively links capitalism, democracy, and individualism. I buy, therefore I am.

For example, buying a Kim Kardashian fragrance performs several functions: not only does it verify and augment Kim's celebrity as well as raise her profits, for the consumer it connotes a set of meanings pertaining to Kim's image, which may transition from Kim to the consumer through merchandise. Moreover, the action of commodifying Kim's image and the act of purchasing supports the ideology of capitalism, linking capitalism, consumerism, social identity, and celebrity.

Celebrity as Commodity

The third means of defining celebrity is by viewing it solely as a commodity, or product designed to be sold. Celebrity "is an industry just like any other, except that instead of making cars, they manufacture bottle-blond pop stars" (Piazza, 2011, p. 15). Historically, Hollywood celebrities have typically always been associated with commodification and the promotion of consumerism (De Cordova, 1990). Consumer demand creates celebrities: "Celebrities are commodities bought and sold by their fans" (Piazza, 2011, p. 15).

Celebrity is created by the work of many: agents, publicists, managers, stylists, etc. These celebrity industry workers, whom Rojek (2001) labels "cultural intermediaries" help "concoct the public presentation of celebrity" (p. 11). Rein et al. (1997) explicate the difference between several industries, all of which participate in the business of celebrity. The communication industry, which includes newspapers, magazines, radio, etc., interacts with the publicity industry, composed of publicists, public relations and advertising agencies, and market research firms. This industry engages with the representation industry, which includes agents, managers, and promoters. Celebrity image is aided by the appearance industry, which includes makeup artists, stylists, and fashion designers, as well as interior designers. Rein et al. (1997) assert the endorsement industry is also part of celebrity, including those who manufacture merchandise as well as the legal and business services industries. Missing from this catalog is social media, which is a new industry unto itself. Companies like Ad.ly match celebrities and products for social media promotion. Turner (2004) also points out that branding specialists and ancillary products utilizing celebrity to sell products are absent from Rein's list. Kim Kardashian and her family are an exemplar of the confluence of all these celebrity industries.

Fame is symbiotic for all parties and varied industries involved. These "economic interdependencies" rely on celebrity (Turner, 2004). As such, *US Weekly* needs to sell magazines, thus wants Kim on the cover. Kim wants to be on the cover to amplify her fame. Turner (2004) notes these interdependencies are kept shrouded from the public in order to sell advertising as news. The benefits multiple parties: the publicist, the journalist, the magazine, and the celebrity. It also behooves the press contingent upon celebrity for revenue to usually treat celebrities kindly. Rein et al. (1997) aver that up to seventy percent of all news originates in the public relations industry. It's no surprise that when Kim Kardashian separated from husband Kris Humphries, celebrity-based magazines placed the break-up blame squarely upon his shoulders.

While stars may be ostensibly publicizing movies, television shows, etc., they are essentially selling themselves, revealing details of lives in order to get audiences to like them. People buy tickets to Jennifer Aniston movies in part to see Jennifer Aniston. The nature of celebrity is the "construction of the individuated personality" (Turner, 2004, p. 37). However, the Hollywood industry is served by any number of interchangeable celebrities. While Jennifer Aniston may be famed for her uniqueness, there could conceivably be many more actresses like her who could sell the movie as well. Aniston must always fight to maintain her relevance, and she does this by maintaining a presence in the public eye.

As Turner noted, "once achieved, of course, celebrity can spin-off into many related sub-industries through endorsements, merchandising, and so on" (2004, p. 39). These endorsements can produce the bulk of a celebrity's income. At least 25 percent of all American ads include celebrity endorsement (Money, Shimp, & Sakano, 2006). Rein et al. (1997) maintain that sports stars often earn up to two-thirds of their income from fame-derived industries, such as sneaker endorsements.

Brands often consist of a celebrity's identity, which in turn is then associated with products. Indeed, "brand creation allows stars to make products based solely on their identity" (Currid-Halkett, 2010, p. 182). Piazza asserted, "as with any commodity, a celebrity's value is determined in the marketplace by the consumer. A brand is all of that intangible stuff that makes consumers want a commodity" (2011, pp. 15-16)

Part of a successful brand is determining what audiences admire most about a celebrity and then matching products to that attribute. This succeeds because "we buy products if they are plausible extensions of stars" (Currid-Halkett, 2010, pp. 183-184).

Symbiotically, products, endorsements, and branding in turn amplify celebrity by making a celebrity ubiquitous. This follows Boorstin's tautology; the more present a person is throughout media, the more famous he or she becomes. The celebrity commodification raises the celebrity profile, as well the amount in his or her bank account.

Reality-TV stars are the most recent celebrities to join the celebrity-as-brands commodification: "Today, though widely considered D-list celebrities, they [reality TV celebrities] are sought after for lucrative endorsement deals, can dictate their salaries, and often earn more per year than A-list movie stars" (Piazza, 2011, p. 43). Reality stars also obtain brand endorsements because of

> how cheap they are in comparison to move stars or established television stars. A brand can't sign an endorsement package with a movie star for under $1 million, but a reality star would accept a tenth of that. Brands also found that consumers related better to reality stars than they did to movie and traditional television actors (Piazza, 2011, p. 55).

The famous must constantly work, as "capitalism can never permit desire to be fulfilled, since to do so will neutralize desire and thus, forfeit economic growth" (Rojek, 2001, p. 189). This unceasing desire to consume (fostered by the famous), is harmful to self-identity, as this lust can never be satiated. Redmond (2006) disagrees, in that for a limited time, buying a product "increases one's self-worth and self-esteem, when one feels empowered by the thing, more alive than one did before it was possessed" (p. 39).

Celebrity brands and celebrity display of wealth promote the idea that satisfaction is attained through consumerism. As Redmond asserts "the commodified celebrity peddles the myth of the autonomous individual and the value of consumption for a full and happy life" (2006, pp. 38-39). The Kardashians exemplify this ideal, that happiness can be bought though designer clothing, diamond jewelry, and expensive cars. However, happiness and wealth do not have a sustainable link over time (Jhally, 2006). Additionally, while the Kardashians may represent the pinnacle of consumption, to audiences this may be "consumer behavior as a means of constructing the everydayness, their similarity to 'us'" (Turner, 2004, p. 41). Finally, the series illustrates an important aspect of the Kardashian image: celebrity attainment and maintenance.

Narcissism/Celebrity

A primary dichotomy within *Keeping Up with the Kardashians* is the inter-woven relationship between celebrity and narcissism. The family members are striving for celebrity, which often both requires and engenders narcissism. However, the family members decry megalomania as an unwelcome trait, setting up a conflict between the desire for fame and presumption of entitlement. The first episode of season two is titled *Kim Becomes a Diva*, implying the negative association between celebrity and arrogance, despite the fact the Kardashians all aspire to attain renown. The initial exchange of the episode follows:

> Kim says, "Did you guys know that I'm like the number one Google search last week?"
> Khloé replies, "Oh my god Kim, shut up. You're so into yourself."
> Kim rejoins, "And then yesterday, I was the top AOL search for the whole week."
> Kourtney asks, "Did you also know, you are number two on the dumbest people list, for the *New York Post*?"
> Kim retorts, "As long as they're talking about me, honey."

The presence of celebrity in the verbal and visual discourse within the series corresponds with Turner's (2004) conception of celebrity as a product of discourse. That the Kardashians are celebrities is averred throughout the discourse in a variety of means, including by associating with famous friends. For example, guests at Khloé's season four wedding to Lamar Odom included Kelly Osbourne, Phil Jackson, Ryan Seacrest, and Kobe Bryant, among others. Other celebrities appearing throughout the series include athletes like tennis player Serena Williams, boxer Sugar Ray Lenard, and NBA player Rashad McCants; other reality TV participants such as Brittny Gastineau and Jonathan Cheban; random minor celebrities, for example one of Jennifer Lopez's ex-husbands, acclaimed choreographer Cris Judd. In season six, guests attending Kim and Kris Humphries's wedding included Eva Longoria, Kathie Lee Gifford, Cheryl Burke, Mark Ballas, Mario Lopez, Ciara, Carmelo Anthony, La La Vasquez, Demi Lovato, Babyface, Scottie Pippen, and musician The Dream. Kim's boyfriend during the early seasons, Reggie Bush, maintains his own fame, which duly impresses Kim even as she associates herself with it. Her season seven boyfriend, musician Kanye West, is a global musical celebrity.

The spoken and visual discourse, particularly centered upon Kim, also connotes celebrity status and its partner, narcissism. Examples abound; for instance, Khloé's blind date asks if Kim Kardashian is her sister, connoting that other people recognize Kim as famous (S2, E5). Additionally, Kim is frequently shown on red carpets and the center of photo-shoots. However, narcissism is the partner of celebrity. On one occasion, Rob finds Kim constructing a photo album that consists solely of shots of herself (S3, E2).

Cultural intermediaries (such as managers, publicists, make-up artists, etc.) help facilitate the construction of celebrity (Rojek, 2001). In season three, Kim explains in her camera narrative that she's busy and thus requires stylists to coordinate her outfits (S3, E11). Personal stylists, formulating outfits consisting of dresses, shoes, and accessories intended to be worn on television and red carpets, typically work for celebrities or the very wealthy, signifying Kim's rank. The episode shows each stylist-chosen outfit in a garment bag labeled with an event, such as a *TV Guide* party, and appearances on Chelsea Handler's show and *Extra*. In a fit of egocentricity, Kim is angered when Kourtney borrows items the stylists had chosen for Kim, even though she clearly has more than enough clothes. The sisters reconcile after the spat, with Kim rewarding Kourtney for apologizing by bringing her to the *TV Guide* party (and its red carpet, replete with photographers) and permitting her to wear the more flattering dress. Other family members' celebrity is manifested in other ways; for example, newlyweds Khloé and Lamar choose to appear on *Chelsea Lately* for their first joint appearance.

One of the issues that estrange Kim and Kris Humphries is her need for fame and his discomfort with it, illustrated by an experience lunching at a restaurant. A gaggle of photographers greet them as they exit their car and then flash their cameras through the front window, visibly watching Kim and Humphries eat. Humphries reveals his discomfort to Kim, which worries her. While Humphries may dislike the press intrusion, for Kim, photographers and fans are normal and desired. As Kim reacts in dismay, Humphries suggests they move to his Minnesota hometown and start having babies. Kim rejoins by observing that his understanding of her career is a reason she loves him.

At Humphries's Las Vegas bachelor party, he discusses the issue of celebrity with his brother-in-law, Lamar Odom. The two converse in a nightclub crammed with revelers, all straining to get a glimpse, or photo, of the bachelor party. Humphries, gesturing toward the crowd—representative of fame and popularity—tells Lamar that this is his world. Lamar retorts that this is now Humphries's world as well. Humphries explains he avoids the paparazzi, while Lamar astutely replies that if Humphries wants celebrity and its trappings, it's there for him (S6, E14).

Fiscal compensation is an important characteristic of celebrity. In season two, Rob, continually searching for a career and income, decides he wants to model. He notes that Kim profits from her modeling and asks for her advice (S2, E6). In this instance, as in others, Rob tries to benefit financially from his celebrity. Another family member, mom Kris, can only see celebrity in terms of money. During season two, Kim makes a sexy calendar for boyfriend Reggie Bush, intending it for his eyes only. Kris finds it and assumes it's her job to place the calendar in retail outlets, which she accordingly does. Kim ruefully notes that her mother attempts to commercialize Kim's thoughtful gift (S2, E9).

Approximately once per season the Kardashians utilize their celebrity for a charity event, which also affirms their celebrity standing. For example, in season four the family boxes for the benefit of the American Heart Foundation; in season two various family members attend a celebrity pool tournament raising money for Hurricane Katrina victims. While in New Orleans for the event, the sisters are approached by an apparently arbitrary family. The family's daughter explains they live in a Federal Emergency Management Agency trailer, having lost their home in Hurricane Katrina. The Kardashians visit their FEMA trailer, present the family with furniture for their new home, and treat them to a fancy dinner, while Reggie Bush gifts football tickets (S2, E10). This interaction seemingly demonstrates the Kardashians' magnanimity, while the stark differences between the poor, non-famous, and African-American family and the Kardashians reifies their privileged rank.

While the discourse confirms that Kim is the most famous Kardashian, the series also emphasizes that the family must join together to promote individual members and thus the family itself, to the advantage of the Kardashian celebrity, brand, and financial status. Accordingly, the entire family attends a party celebrating an issue of local California magazine *944* featuring Kourtney on the cover (S3, E5). The family must all participate in order to achieve success. When Bruce wants to leave the party early, Kris chastises him, referring to her total family involvement credo. This philosophy was adopted from the start of her media career and exemplified by the entire family appearing in Kris and Bruce's early gym infomercials. The whole of the family is greater than the sum of its parts. This is also illustrated by the presence of family members in the various spin-offs. The Kardashian brand is comprised of all the Kardashians together.

The family must continually work, together and separately, to maintain celebrity. Once they are out of the spotlight, their fame will recede as well. This corresponds with Rojek's (2001) assertion that once desire is fulfilled, or a product purchased, the capitalistic engine will cease. The Kardashians must consistently create new products to create a need to consume for their fans; hence the seemingly unceasing-cycle of new series and products. Becoming stagnant, or fading from the limelight, would reduce the amount of Kardashian media impressions and subsequently their fame. Accordingly, the amount of Kardashian family members aids them. When the audience presumably tires of Kim, a program starring Kourtney and Khloé may air. In this way, a Kardashian celebrity/commodified persona generally remains in the media discourse, guaranteeing name recognition for all.

The Kardashian celebrity is a brand unto itself; as a whole, they are not simply a family but a commodity, selling products they've created and merchandise they endorse. The show facilitates this celebrity by asserting they are indeed famous from the very start of the program. *Keeping Up with the Kardashians* is the centerpiece of their brand empire, providing the basis of celebrity maintenance through its depictions.

BEAUTY/UNHAPPINESS

Celebrities represent dominant cultural meanings. On reality TV, the primary female beauty characteristics are youth, whiteness, thinness, surgical alteration, and hypersexuality (Pozner, 2010). Celebrity standards also accord with these attributes. While the program pays lip service to the concept of accepting all body types, *Keeping Up with the Kardashians* reifies stereotypical beauty qualities, while complicating the issue of beauty norms through the depiction of another duality: beauty and unhappiness.

The Kardashian women exemplify almost a caricature of femininity and the female form. This is illustrated through lengthy hair extensions, hourglass figures exaggerated through tight, fashionable designer clothing, sky-high heels, huge eyes encircled with dramatically heavy makeup, and darkly tanned skin. The Kardashian sisters epitomize a level of physical appearance that most people cannot possibly achieve. The at-home audience views them barely working to achieve this beauty, endorsing the message that by the work depicted, this beauty is attainable. However, labor exists: exercising, dieting, and frequently cosmetic surgery. What the audience does witness promotes the goal of perfection, seemingly achievable through the little work actually portrayed. The Kardashians perform the labor of having their lives recorded for which they receive payment. Like the majority of people appearing on television, they simply exist resplendent in their beauty, without the audience seeing the majority of preparation involved. While the Kardashian family members seemingly embrace their full-figured curves, their discourse indicates a preference for the societal norm of a lithe shape. In tandem with the beauty message within the show is the idea that beauty does not equal happiness or confidence. The very first words of the first episode are this exchange:

> Kim complains: "I'm starving."
> Khloé responds: "Don't you have a photo shoot tomorrow? Stop eating."
> Kris then whispers to Khloé: "I think she has a little junk in the trunk. The jiggles."

Other family members laugh in the background, implicitly bolstering the idea of beauty requiring a svelte figure. Later in the season, Kim complains of invisible cellulite on her stomach during a bikini photo shoot. Examples of this type are myriad throughout the show; they emphasize physical appearance norms, while sowing jealousy, insecurity, and family discord.

In another symptomatic sequence, while preparing for Tyra Banks's talk show, Kim has false eyelashes applied, her hair professionally styled, and tries on several outfits and pairs of high heels. Simultaneously, she confesses her anxiety about appearing on the show. Kim's superficial appearance is an accomplishment that takes a team of people, several hours, and thousands of dollars, with apparently little work actually done by her. Paradoxically, after all this beauty pampering, insecure and nervous, Kim looks into the camera and tearfully wishes for her sisters presence.

Kim's unhappiness juxtaposed with her physical appearance exemplifies a conflict: beauty norms and the supposed happiness of being considered attractive, contrasted with the pressure of the aforementioned norms and celebrity.

In season two, episode nine, Kim decides to feature herself in a sexy calendar as a gift for boyfriend Reggie. Before the photo-shoot, in which she wears skimpy lingerie and scanty costumes, she brings Kourtney and Khloé with her to a visit to the plastic surgeon. Kim justifies this visit, claiming that even with working out all the time, she still has cellulite. The doctor uses a VelaShape machine on Kim, a device intended to reduce the appearance of cellulite, which sucks at Kim's thighs, sides, and rear end. The credits of this episode note VelaShape supplied promotional consideration (read: product placement fee). VelaShape also appears in season three, when Khloé receives the treatment. Regardless of product placement, the use of this body enhancement procedure still suggests a concern with an unattainable body image.

Plastic surgery is often mentioned on the series and is utilized at various times by sundry family members. For example, Kourtney openly discusses her breast implants in various episodes, Kim receives Botox injections (S5, E5), and both Kris and Bruce indulge in appearance rejuvenation (S3, E10). Kris undergoes a face-lift (S6, E14) and has breast enhancement surgery (S7, E17). These procedures correspond with American youthful beauty norms.

Putting her own surgery ambitions aside temporarily, Kris focuses on persuading Bruce to get a facelift in order to correct previously botched work (S3, E10). According to Kris, the bungled 1984 facelift and nose job contribute to Bruce's low self-esteem. At-home viewers are shown a 1976 photo of Bruce, looking young and handsome and noticeably different from his clearly altered current look. Bruce complains about his treatment by the media in regard to his plastic surgery, averring that websites and magazines lambast him. Kris pressures him to seek a doctor's help, convincing him to visit Dr. Garth Fisher, a plastic surgeon and family friend.

At the doctor's office, Bruce expounds upon his love/hate relationship with the media, disclosing that 1980s media outlets criticized him, including him on worst plastic surgeries lists. While Bruce may lament his perceived lampooning by the media, he needs media attention to extend his celebrity and career. He may claim to be unintentionally courting media through his participation in reality television, but he is pandering to them nevertheless through publicity-seeking promotional events.

Bruce worries that the media would deride him if he submits to plastic surgery again, which also indicates an inflated sense of celebrity and importance. Perhaps this worry about the media is a manifestation of fear about further altering his face in an unattractive way. He is initially quite vehement in his refusal of surgeries, but Kris preys upon his insecurities, convincing him to aspire to conventional beauty ideals of youth and wrinkle-free skin. Finally, Kris's incessant appeals to his vanity and utilization of his low self-esteem manipulate him into surgery.

During the eight or nine hour surgery, the family waits at the hospital and the audience sees the gruesome operation: doctors cut his skin from his skull, peel his eyelids back, and blood wells up. The grisly details are unexpected and shocking to see in a family-oriented program, even one that frequently uses explicit language, and highlight the extreme lengths the family members will go in the efforts to achieve and conform to beauty norms.

Kim's season six wedding is another reason for plastic surgery. Kris claims to dislike her supposed jowls and expresses her unhappiness with her face. Bruce thinks Kris is obsessing about herself, and while Kris agrees, she won't stop focusing on her looks. One of the many details about the wedding Kris can control is her appearance (S6, E14). Later, reflecting on the facelift surgery, Kris discusses years of being self-conscious about her neck, chin, and body, followed by a montage of insecure moments depicted in past years' shows, such as one in which Kris asks Kim if she looks fat.

The Kardashian sisters have mixed emotions about their mother's surgery. Kim contends that Khloé and Kourtney are too nonchalant about the surgery, while Kim is concerned about possible complications. During the surgery itself, the sisters have a scheduled photo-shoot, in which they breezily participate, with only Kim seemingly worried about the surgery. The viewing audience is treated to graphic images of Kris's surgery: sections of skin are marked, cut, and lifted from her face. Afterwards, Kris lies drugged in a hotel room, attached to a nearby IV, her face and neck wrapped in bandages, unable to move. Kim spends the night on a cot next to the hotel bed. After the reveal, in which Kris looks essentially the same as she did before the surgery, the family relates how proud they are of their mother's appearance (S6, E14). Surgery and the accompanying pain are apparently inconsequential in the pursuit of beauty ideals.

In a similar event, the next season Kris casually informs Kendall and Kylie she's having her breast implants redone (S7, E17). By 2012, twenty-three years after her original breast augmentation, according to Kris, her size D breasts are too big and out of current fashion. At her meeting with the plastic surgeon, Kris jokes about posing for *Playboy* post-operation, while the doctor's assistant appears aghast. As Kris drifts into an anesthetized sleep, viewers see the hands on a clock pass, Kris on a surgery table, and the old implants and the new ones. Post-surgery, Kris invites the family over to see her surgery results. Her kids react in horror at her offer to see her breasts, while Scott jokes. The Kardashians take plastic surgery in stride; nothing seems to faze them, particularly risky procedures undertaken in order to match standards of beauty. A 56-year-old woman endeavoring to fit into designer clothes and attain the perky breasts of a younger woman is treated as normal and given no in-depth consideration. This corresponds with Pozner's (2010) contention that reality TV naturalizes plastic surgery and unrealistic standards of beauty.

Throughout the series, people will occasionally discuss the need to eat healthily, which when considered in conjunction with the emphasis on weight and body image, is truly a euphemism for the need to diet into thinness. On the second episode of season two, Kris chastises Kim for eating cake and desserts. She then hires a nutritionist to educate the family about dining in a healthful way. This conceit is echoed in season four, when Kendall becomes a model (S4, E8). Kris says to Kendall: "If you're gonna be a model you've got to have good nutrition. You know what I'm saying?" While a mother wanting her family to eat better is laudable, the conflation of her mother and manager roles hints at a more nefarious reason for controlling her children's diets: in Hollywood, fat clients receive less work, fewer endorsements, and fewer opportunities.

Throughout the series, Khloé copes with body image unhappiness and insecurity. Adding to her self-doubt, the family often jokes about her being overweight and larger than her sisters. When asked to pose nude for PETA (S4, E3), Khloé expresses anxiety about her size, referring to herself as an obese fat cow and a gorilla. Kourtney tells the camera that media comparisons between the sisters are unfair; Kim and Kourtney are petite, standing about 5 feet tall, while Khloé is 5 foot 9. The sisters contend that the media often ridicule Khloé; on the episode, she reads a celebrity gossip website that labels her a beast and likens her to a man.

Khloé worries about posing nude for PETA's "I'd rather go naked than wear fur campaign," expressing her doubts if she's the kind of girl who can pose naked. Following this admission, a montage plays of previous PETA campaign spots featuring Eva Mendes, Pamela Anderson, and model Christy Turlington.

The show discourse stresses a perfect body while paying lip service to the idea that everyone should be happy with his or her natural appearance. While Khloé can express discontent with her physical appearance, she gets upset when someone else mentions it to her. In this episode, Bruce asks Khloé:

"don't you think you could lose a few pounds?" Khloé responds by angrily exiting the room.

In this indicative illustration, within this body-image-focused episode the perfect physique is emphasized throughout program discourse via body-image anxiety and visual nudity prominence. Additionally, fans of the show may also be aware of the family's endorsement of an appetite suppressant line, which also highlights the importance of bodily perfection.

At the actual photo-shoot, when Khloé is required to take off her clothes and pose nude, she runs off set, unable to drop her robe, and refers to herself as Kim Kardashian's fat, funny sister. Ultimately, she is convinced to disrobe and the shoot is accomplished. At the end of the episode the clearly retouched image is revealed and Khloé reflects upon the experience: "People need to know you have to embrace your curves and embrace everything and love who you are."

Khloé's brief, politically-correct final thought on body acceptance is belied by the body dismorphia and unhappy discourse of the previous 20 minutes (as well as other episodes' discourse). The intense self-loathing far outweighs the compendiary addendum.

Interestingly, while the mainstream press and other Kardashian media often feature stories focused on the Kardashian sisters' body image, *Kim Kardashian's Fairytale Wedding* features a plot line revolving around Rob's weight (S6, E14). Before the wedding, the family points out that Rob has gained around 30 pounds. Khloé warns Rob, who lives with Khloé and Lamar, that he'll look bloated at the wedding if he persists in eating poorly. The concern about Rob's weight isn't for health reasons; it's for his appearance.

Khloé and Lamar's pantry is well stocked with chips, cookies, doughnuts, candy, and other high-sugar and fatty snack food that Lamar enjoys eating. In order to catch Rob secretly binge eating junk food, Khloé installs a large gadget that emits a squealing noise as the pantry door is opened. Later that night, the screeching noise is heard and Lamar and Khloé confront Rob. In shame, Rob blames Khloé and Lamar for having junk food in the house.

Rob then moves in with Scott and Kourtney, who live a healthy lifestyle. Despite living with them, Rob visits a fast food restaurant and gorges on fatty food. Kourtney finds the fast food trash in her kitchen and explains to Rob, "Be responsible. You're an adult—you can eat whatever you want" (S6, E14). By the end of the episode, Rob has moved back in with Khloé and Lamar and admits to binge eating. Just like his sisters, Rob feels societal and familial pressure to lose weight.

This superficial distress about appearances supports beauty stereotypes; namely, that women need to look youthful and have taut skin and a firm body. However, the plotline concerning Rob's weight signifies the beauty ideal of thinness for men as well as women. These dual plotlines support existent beauty norms. Rob enjoys eating, but is not allowed to, for fear his weight will be detrimental not to his health, but to his and the Kardashian image, an anxiety echoed in other episodes centered upon Rob's weight as well. *Keeping Up with the Kardashians* is unique in this regard; men are not typically featured on television as struggling to maintain beauty-focused cultural norms.

The dominant meaning expressed throughout this beauty/unhappiness dichotomy is that adherence to conventional appearance norms is extremely important and moreover, that beauty is attainable with money. There is an emphasis on conventional beauty ideals, visible through family members' plastic surgeon visits and Khloé's despondency about her body not conforming to beauty ideals. The show-normalized body-altering procedures are contra to the idea of being happy with your body or actually working to alter it. Their celebrity status and ubiquity throughout media encourages consumers to covet the Kardashian image, which includes the Kardashian endorsement of body enhancing devices like VelaShape and similar treatments. This connotes that anyone can look like a Kardashian by buying Kardashian-designed clothes, spraying Kardashian-endorsed perfume, and using VelaShape.

However, as media texts are polysemic (Dyer, 1986/2004), other meanings pertaining to body image and beauty may be ascertained from the series, notably stemming from the discontent paired with beauty. This misery that the Kardashians exhibit complicates the beauty benchmarks. A secondary interpretation may be that despite money, surgery, etc., happiness attained via beauty is never achievable. Despite promises made by surgery and cosmetics, the struggle to reach celebrity standards is perpetual. This meaning aligns with the capitalistic need to continually instill the itch to consume, scratched by new products; the Kardashians unending search for the perfect products and procedures to attain acceptable beauty demonstrates capitalism's facilitation of the urge to consume.

SEXUAL/CONSERVATIVE

Celebrities, in addition to representing beauty standards, embody sexuality norms as well. In media, even within family-oriented programming, sexual objectification of women is a norm (Wood, 2011). For example, in advertising that includes women, sexuality is often the most important element (Jhally, 2006). Wood noted that "media repeat the cultural view of women as dependent, ornamental objects who exist to look good, to please men, to care for children, and to be sexually desirable and available" (2011, p. 265). Youthful, thin women are the norm (Harrison, 2008).

Furthermore, "reality TV is particularly strong in reinforcing traditional views of women and what makes women desirable" (Wood, 2011, p. 265). Shows like *America's Next Top Model*, *Extreme Makeover*, and *What Not To Wear* highlight traditional beauty valuations of thinness, whiteness, and sexualization. Wood asserts that "the message for women is clear: Your worth is based on your sexuality; if you aren't super-hot, you must transform yourself" (2011, p. 265). Douglas (2010) notes on reality TV, the most important rule is that "women are to be judged first and foremost by their appearance" (p. 198). Women are encouraged to be sexual, feminine, and passive, as corresponds to cultural feminine ideals, yet then objectified for these qualities (Jhally & Katz, 2001; Wood, 2011).

On reality TV, commodified sexuality is particularly prominent (Lundy, Ruth, & Park, 2008). Programs like *The Bachelor*, *Rock of Love*, *The Girls Next Door*, and *Keeping Up with the Kardashians* represent women utilizing sexuality in order to achieve goals (Wood, 2011). The commodification of this hypersexuality implies that the average women can attain this sexuality and associated beauty through consumption of beauty products and goods (Gill, 2008; McRobbie, 2004).

Keeping Up with the Kardashians exhibits a paradox of conservative family-first values with an image of overt sexuality. While the sisters often appear explicitly sexualized in popular media, verbal discourse of the show emphasizes conservative values, such as fidelity, stability, and marriage. Whereas Kim earned fame from her supposedly privately-filmed pornographic recording, on the show she is hesitant and dubious of posing for *Playboy* (S1, E4). Kim's initial reaction to the magazine's offer is incredulity, and wants to turn down the offer.

However, after debating whether or not to say yes, Kim decides to pose for the magazine with the caveat that she will not be photographed fully nude. *Playboy* is unhappy with the resultant images and requires more skin to be shown, necessitating a second, more sexual photoshoot. Despite Kim's doubtful and insecure portrayal, once in front of the *Playboy* camera again, she sexily poses, arches her back, and appears almost fully nude, bare save for strands of pearls.

While superficial overt sexuality standards (such as skimpy clothing and nudity) are often considered negative in real life (although oft celebrated in media), on the show these norms are depicted as neutral, if not positive. However, these sexuality norms may be dangerous, as evidenced by the family's attempts to shield Kylie and Kendall from them. On a telling occasion, one of the little girls entered the kitchen while Kourtney, Khloé, Kim, and Kris were perusing Kim's images from the Playboy shoot. Rob picked up the child and carried the little girl out of the room (S1, E4). The family acknowledges the younger girls should be protected, while the older sisters exploit their sexuality in order to earn fame and monetary rewards.

Kim's superficial concern about her sexualized image, when anyone can buy her pornographic video, is extremely ironic. Moreover, she capitalizes on her body, posing practically nude for magazines, calendars, and other merchandise, and often appears in public provocatively dressed. This contradiction between vocalized conservative values and outward image may provoke fascination and is perhaps cultivated to make Kim appeal to both men (who may appreciate her figure) and women (who possibly may appreciate her verbal value system). Kim has created an image that is both the Madonna and whore. This image exemplifies the many powerful and contradictory media messages present within popular culture.

Two cultural imperatives coexist within media for women: "sexuality is everything" and "good girls don't" (Jhally & Katz, 2001, p. 30). While the "virgin" and the "whore" date back to biblical times, in contemporary culture women are expected to be both highly sexualized and virginal. Kim Kardashian represents this paradox; she is highly sexualized, yet professes to adhere to the values of fidelity and temperance. She doesn't drink, doesn't do drugs, and is a serial monogamist, yet retains an extremely sexualized image.

Douglas (2010) contends that mediated sexual images are prevalent throughout post-2000 media due to the presence of their antitheses, strong heroines. Her phrase "enlightened sexism" speaks to the supposed achievement of equality, symbolized by heroines like *Buffy the Vampire Slayer* and *Xena, Warrior Princess*. Since these depictions exist, it's also acceptable to "resurrect sexist stereotypes of girls and women" (2010, p. 9). As women now "have it all" they can "focus the bulk of their time and energy on their appearance, pleasing men, being hot, competing with other women, and shopping" (2010, p. 10). Reality TV is a hotbed of "contrived egalitarianism" (2010, p. 189). While the Kardashians' sexual depictions throughout various media may appear to represent enlightened sexism, their ownership of their business empire complicates this notion. In addition, although they may portray and maintain sexual standards, other concomitant values throughout the series mitigate the dominance of this illustration.

In a sense, Kim Kardashian may represent Angela McRobbie's (2009) conception of post-feminism, in which women have given up their claims to feministic equality in exchange for a discourse of individualism. As women make strides in workplace equality and self-empowerment, the focus on beauty functions to maintain heterosexual and beauty norms. Individualism concentrates upon the power of public femininity, placing emphasis on physical beauty and the commercial consumption necessary to maintain it. Subsequently, with the power given to it, the "global fashion-beauty complex charges itself with the business of ensuring that appropriate gender relations are guaranteed" (McRobbie, 2009, p. 61). In this way, industry and government mitigate feminism. As Kim profits from her sexual image, she exemplifies a contortion of feminism; she benefits from her own exploitation.

CONSPICUOUS CONSUMPTION

The Kardashians are active participants in the capitalistic economy, hawking wares and themselves through multiple forms of media. In this process, they buttress notions of materialism and consumerism. Materialism is the notion that having nicer, current things makes you better than others; consumerism is the idea that buying goods engenders self-worth in some form. Materialism fosters consumerism. Materialism is thus the high *valuation* of expensive items; owning them makes you an inherently better person than someone who does not. Consumerism is the idea that *buying something fixes you in some way*, also consequently nurturing capitalism.

American media, as part of the capitalistic establishment, promote consumerism, urging consumers to buy more and more merchandise. This is accomplished by persuading audiences that owning the right product will allow the consumer to be cool and happy (Levin & Kilbourne, 2008; Steyer, 2003). Douglas (2010) contends the millennial generation, in particular, are repeatedly assured that purchasing the right brands will assure power. Moreover, more than other genres of television, reality TV contends that items are not luxuries but necessities (Pozner, 2010).

In Twitchell's (1999) celebration of consumer culture, *Lead Us Into Temptation: The Triumph of American Materialism*, he notes that objects themselves have no meaning other than function; advertisers add value and significance to objects through branding. In an American culture devoid of religiosity, Americans buy goods in order to give their lives meaning (Twitchell, 1999). In fact, at no other point in history have people been able to buy so much, for so little money. Twitchell's main argument is that "branding, packaging, fashion, and even the act of shopping itself are now the central meaning-making acts in our postmodern world" (1999, p. 14).

Symbolically, materialism democratically binds Americans. The American dream posits that anyone may achieve success and wealth, accomplishing the goal of attaining the ability to buy whatever one wants. This helps augment national identity.

One of the earliest works on materialism within American culture is the seminal 1899 book *The Theory of the Leisure Class* by Thorstein Veblen. In this book, Veblen coins the term "conspicuous consumption," referring to the affluent ostentatiously owning luxurious material goods in order to "advertise their wealth, thereby achieving greater social status" (Bagwell & Bernheim, 1996, p. 349). Status is gained and demonstrated to peers through accumulation of costly material goods. Consumers are motivated to conspicuously consume for two reasons: "invidious comparison" and "pecuniary emulation" (Veblen, 1899/1994). Veblen postulates that members of upper socioeconomic classes invidiously compare in order to differentiate themselves from lower socioeconomic class members. Similarly, lower socioeconomic class members engage in pecuniary emulation in order to pose as a member of a higher socioeconomic class.

The term conspicuous consumption and its corollaries, invidious comparison and pecuniary emulation, are utilized by heterogeneous academic fields. For example, within economics, "'Veblen effects' are said to exist when consumers exhibit a willingness to pay a higher price for a functionally equivalent good" (Bagwell & Bernheim, 1996, p. 349). Bagwell and Bernheim (1996) suggest that much merchandise is priced higher simply to induce Veblen effects.

The Kardashians compulsively consume, opting for high-cost and high-status goods, as demonstrated throughout the television series. This conspicuous consumption lends itself readily to product endorsement, in which the Kardashian brand and image attributes are transferred to a product. This is how much advertising works: by reallocating a concept from one entity to another (Williamson, 1978). Perhaps the most glaring example of Kardashian conspicuous consumption was Kim Kardashian's over-the-top wedding. The Kardashians exhibit their consumption on their TV series, as well as in social media.

Theme: Materialism

Throughout the series, there is an emphasis concerning materialism; the Kardashians live an ostentatious lifestyle, replete with expensive cars, gigantic mansions, and exotic vacations. On the first episode of the first season, Kim explains her family thusly: "There's a lot of baggage that comes with us. But it's like Louis Vuitton baggage; you always want it."

As one journalist noted, a draw for audiences is the "nonstop fabulosity of the family's lifestyle: the size of Khloé's engagement ring, the houses and clothes, the cars, the clubs, the swimming pools, the collection of dishes (Hermès), the humongous diamond studs in Rob's ears, the private jets" (Merkin, 2010, para 7). Indeed, the houses featured on the show are incredible, particularly the second family mansion, featured on seasons three through seven. Although the first home on the series is casually referenced to being worth 20 million dollars at one point (S2, E2) it was listed for sale in 2008 for $3,395,000 (Brenoff, 2008). After the initial success of the show, the family moved into a new, gigantic house in the exclusive Hidden Hills neighborhood of Calabasas, California, featuring marble floors, Jacuzzi tubs, chandeliers, and flat screen TVs throughout. As their fortune increases, so does the trappings of their wealth; houses become mansions, Ferraris replace Mercedes, and dinners are created by private chefs, not family members. To reiterate, materialism is valuing expensive items because owning them makes you better than your peers. Consumerism is the idea that buying something betters you as a person. As Veblen asserted (1899/1994) conspicuously consuming elevates class status. It is worth noting that according to typical standards, the Kardashians have always been wealthy. In her memoir, Kris Jenner recalls Robert Kardashian driving a Rolls Royce on dates. However, their recent financial success has put them into an even higher socioeconomic bracket. Their lifestyle is in accordance with this achievement.

One of the themes throughout the series, as stated in the very title of the show, is keeping up, as in the cliché of "keeping up with the Jones" or maintaining an image of wealth. Kourtney asserts if one of Kris's "Beverly Hills friends" has something, Kris needs it, too (S2, E2). Similarly, when Kris contends Bruce is "anti-fashion," he must be persuaded to buy new clothes (S2, E3). While never explicitly said, Bruce must look good to maintain the family's image of glamor and sophistication. Surprising himself, Bruce enjoys the new clothes and his new look, implying that purchasing new clothes can trigger happiness, that appearances are important, and generally sends the message that consumerism, or buying, is beneficial.

In another example of the Kardashian's grandiose lifestyle, their extravagant vacations are brimming with the outlandish activities of the wealthy, including arriving and departing via private plane. In Breckenridge, Colorado, they go dog sledding; in the Dominican Republic, they shoot skeet; in Santa Barbara, they ride horses; in Bora, Bora, they kayak and scuba dive; in Las Vegas, they stay in the Venetian hotel's 8,000 square foot penthouse suite. In Bora, Bora, Kim cries upon losing an earring she claims is worth $75,000 dollars. Then-boyfriend Kris Humphries chastises her, "I personally would never own anything that if I lost it, I would be that emotional about. It's a material good." He lectures, "don't be so materialistic" (S6, E11).

Kim is continually shopping, implying that extravagant spending is acceptable. In one shopping trip, with a discount, Kim's purchases at a clothing boutique total $19,723 (S3, E3). While the family agrees that Kim "has a shopping problem," the discourse of the series contradicts this idea, as the excessive lifestyle led by the family has never been viewed as problematic either previously or in later episodes. After an intervention concerning her spendthrift habits, Kim contritely agrees to give herself a budget (S3, E3). Lip service is paid to the idea of being fiscally responsible while Kim's glamorous lifestyle, designer clothes, and Bentleys belie this claim. A thirty-second lesson at the end of an episode is again outweighed by the enormity of the discourse contradicting the moral conclusion that materialism and consumerism are admirable.

In another episode, Rob tries to reconcile his ingrained materialistic beliefs, that the ability to purchase goods connotes being better than others, with his lack of income. Having just graduated from college, Rob is unemployed yet neglects to show up for an internship interview Kourtney arranges for him (S3, E6). Rob doesn't want to "waste time" on a minimum wage job and invokes his father's adage of "time is money." However, he feels pressure to consume, borrowing Kim's Bentley to appear as if he has income.

Rob's values do not match with his reality. He supposedly begins interning, although in future episodes, Rob is never depicted as having a conventional forty-hours-per-week internship or job. Instead, he participates in *Dancing With The Stars* and by season seven, is pursuing manufacturing his own line of socks.

There are many off-handed comments and situations that seamlessly blend into the plot points of episodes that connote over-the-top consumerism. Casual mentions of couture designers, informal references to and visibility of high-end clothing, expensive accessories, and extravagant automobiles are endemic within the series. Kendall and Kylie are allowed to borrow Hermes Birkin handbags (retail value upwards of $10,000) from their mother's gigantic walk-in closet. Boyfriends don't just gift jewelry, but send a jeweler with a selection of items from which to choose, and a wedding dress necessitates a visit to Vera Wang's salon, during which the designer herself consults.

When Lamar Odom proposed to Khloé, he gave her a 12.5 carat diamond ring. According to *Glamour* magazine, the average weight of a diamond engagement ring is a little over one carat (Bodgas, 2011). *US Weekly* estimates Khloé's ring cost $850,000 (Khloé Kardashian Loses Her $850,000 Engagement Ring, 2010), while Kim's 20.5 diamond engagement ring given to her by Kris Humphries was estimated at being worth $2 million (Hughes, 2011). Kourtney defines Lamar's proposal as a magical moment and not just due to the love propelling the question but the "amazing diamond rock" (S4, E1).

Khloé and Lamar's wedding episode is rife with consumerism discourse and corollary product placement. Featuring products on the show is an inexpensive means of obtaining merchandise and services—everyone involved seemingly benefits in some way. However, the consumerism featured in the wedding may not send a positive message to viewers, and instead may promote overspending and feelings of insecurity. Kris plans Khloé's perfect wedding, which entails flowers by Mark's Garden and registering at Geary's, a luxury home store in Beverly Hills. While Khloé balks at requesting china place settings that cost $750 each, she happily accepts a couture gown from Vera Wang and a Rolls Royce in which to travel to the wedding. The wedding is lavish and exorbitant, far out of reach for the vast majority of viewers.

In Kim's season six wedding, the extravagance of the wedding is repetitively noted. Every aspect of the wedding is designed to be ostentatious. Having candles at the wedding isn't nice enough; Kim and Humphries design their own candle scents. When choosing the food, they meet for a private tasting with celebrity chef Wolfgang Puck. The bridesmaids receive gifts of Judith Leiber handbags, which Kim helped design. Handbags by the same designer start at $2000 dollars at Bergdorf Goodman and Neiman Marcus department stores. Kim arrives at the wedding in a Maybach Rolls Royce; of course, this is probably fitting for the woman whose primary vehicle is a Bentley. Robin Thicke sings the song for Kim and Humphries's first dance as husband and wife. Earth, Wind and Fire also perform.

Visually, the excess and luxury of the nuptials are emphasized. A beauty team of at least five people hovered over Kim, perfecting her look. As she prepared for the event, the audience sees shots of the guests arriving. Following instructions, guests wore white and the matching décor was completely ivory. Every available inch of space was draped in white fabric: the walls, ceiling, and chairs. Ice sculptures, china, and flowers adorned tables, which also featured Lalique swans as ornamentation.

As Kim walked down the aisle glittering in diamond jewelry, the cameras focused on the sumptuous setting: rows and rows of chairs covered in white drapery, celebrities, large bouquets of white flowers, a ten-tier wedding cake, and an ostentatious Swarovski crystal-encrusted cross, over five feet high, anchored to the wall in front of which Kim and Kris stated their vows. Khloé avers, Kim's wedding is "elegant, glamorous, very Zsa Zsa. This is like her fairytale wedding" (S6, E15).

The series features numerous examples of materialism and consumerism, vaunting conscious consumption. This is indicative of the cultural milieu of the time period, where the values that motivate people to buy Rolex watches and Gucci sweaters simultaneously coexist with the motivation to recycle and "go green." Seemingly untouched by the economic explosion of 2008 and the subsequent recession, the Kardashians exemplify a paradox of values, where happiness can be bought in a store, yet family relationships are paramount. These contradictory morals coexist in the illogical world of the Kardashians.

This theme supports the ideology of capitalism. Just as the Kardashians ceaselessly consume, their audience is encouraged to as well, particularly Kardashian products. Conspicuous consumption is overtly linked to the Kardashian brand. They endorse beauty products like their own Khroma cosmetic line, connecting their support of beauty norms to consumption and the ideology of capitalism. Likewise, the celebrity discourse also supports American economics. While ostensibly banal and mindless, reality TV and *Keeping Up with the Kardashians* in particular function to inculcate acquiescence and compliance with capitalism and its directives.

Theme: Hard Work

A corollary to the materialism theme is the theme of hard work. The family consistently talks about their family value of working hard and how frequently they work. They do not discuss the degree of difficulty their jobs entail;

rather, they focus on the time commitment required. Numerous references to how hard they work (read: time spent working) are visible in the series and entire episodes are devoted to Kim and Kris's work ethic.

While it seems as if Bruce never actually works, judging by the time he is shown watching golf, playing with miniature helicopters, and hanging around the house, in season two Khloé and Kourtney travel with him to attend one of Bruce's motivational speaking engagements. Bruce contends, "I work all the time. I'm working hard" (S2, E9).

In contrast, according to the family Scott lacks a work ethic. Upon spying Scott lying by the pool at the Jenner house, Bruce and Kris discuss his perceived laziness. Kris, who is depicted constantly performing her job of manager, notes, "He needs to get a job" (S4, E2).

Another person who spends much of the series without a job is Rob, as discussed earlier. After graduating college, Rob moves back home, where a maid cleans his room, Kris makes him lunch, and he makes use of the pool and Xbox. Bruce is irritated at Rob's lack of work ethic and annoys him into wanting to work simply in order to get out of the house.

However, Bruce is happy Rob graduated college. Bruce explained that before Robert Kardashian, Sr. passed away, he extracted a promise from Bruce to ensure Rob matriculated at the University of Southern California (S2, E6). Strangely enough, this promise only applied to Rob. No such promise was requested for his daughters' benefit and only Kourtney, who applied to college when her father was alive, graduated from college, earning a degree in Theater Arts from the University of Arizona. Neither Kim nor Khloé ever attended college. While hard work, or at least time spent working, is valued, apparently education for women is not.

Theme: Perfect Wedding

At the start of season four, two episodes were devoted to Khloé and Lamar's wedding. In season six, two episodes billed as a special event, with its own title and airing times, were devoted to Kim and Kris Humphries extravagant, made-for-television wedding on August 20, 2011. *Kim Kardashian's Fairytale Wedding* reportedly earned the couple $15 million, aired a repetitious twenty-two times in three weeks, and drew over 4.2 million viewers (Stelter, 2011). And then, a mere seventy-two days after the nuptials, Kim Kardashian announced their separation and imminent divorce. The over-the-top extravaganza represents an extreme version of American culture's fascination with weddings and idealized "perfect endings." The themes of family, celebrity, materialism, and gender roles found throughout the series echo throughout this television special.

The most prevalent narrative throughout the program was that of the perfect wedding, as evidenced in the title of the program. Throughout verbal and visual discourse, the concept of a "fairytale" wedding is repeated. This idealization is elucidated through commentary and visuals, while the definition of a perfect wedding is implicitly assumed to be understood by the audience. This idealized wedding is apparently very stereotypically feminine and centered upon the bride.

Kris claims: "It's all about everything being *way* over the top and spectacular." Correspondingly, Kim agrees her perfect wedding would be the "most glamorous wedding you've ever imagined."

A key aspect of the superlative wedding is the bridal gown. This heteronormative feminine ideal is hegemonically asserted throughout the discourse. According to the program, every woman dreams of a traditional wedding, replete with a white Cinderella-esque ballroom gown. As Kim initially discusses gowns, she examines designer sketches sent from couture designers: Vera Wang, Zac Posen, and Marchesa. She ultimately selects Vera Wang, the quintessential wedding gown designer to create her made-to-order dress, yet cannot choose between three dissimilar dresses. In the end, unable to decide, Kim wears all three.

Referencing a stereotype, Kim asserts that she had been planning this dream wedding since she was a child. Perceptively, Humphries notes that in this case, any man could have been the groom. Kim's planning of the wedding for a long time, before meeting Humphries, supports the idea that women simply want to get married, to any man that will agree.

In a subplot that deflects some attention away from the materialistic components of the wedding, Kim and Humphries visit her father's grave. Humphries reflects on the emotions and familial memories connected to marriage. However, while they're standing at the gravesite, at one point a cameraman's shadow is visible. Kim and Humphries pay lip service to matrimonial ideals of family, love, and loyalty; however, the intensity and amount of wedding preparation scenes overshadow these moralistic values. The bridal-related principles are lost in the clamor and uproar of the wedding. Moreover, the family again commercializes Robert Kardashian's death, using his gravesite as a plot point in the reality program.

While weddings are notoriously expensive, the Kardashian-Humphries affair is ridiculously excessive, extravagant, and over-the-top. Media reported Kim and Kris received at least the "three Vera Wang dresses Kardashian wore during the ceremony and reception, worth $20,000 each, $400,000 in Perrier Jouet Champagne, and $10,000 worth of wedding invitations." Moreover, *People* supposedly paid "$2.5 million for the exclusive rights to wedding photos and a further $300,000 for the engagement shots," while "*OK!* magazine is said to have paid $100,000 for exclusive pictures of the bridal shower." Kim also released a bridal-themed limited edition perfume, named "Love" (Profitable Union).

Considering the ancient history of matrimony, that conventional conceptions of family and gender roles are present is not surprising. Moreover, the focus on an ostentatious and luxurious wedding, when viewed contextually in the scope of history, is also unsurprising. Weddings are traditionally a time for families to display their wealth, to impress their neighbors, and to portray themselves in a positive light. Indeed, the focus on the wedding as a vehicle for celebrity, which is truly what the entire program is implicitly about, also may be viewed as a natural progression in the history of celebrity. Royal weddings have long been occasions for publicity and assertions of superiority.

All the same, no matter the historical cultural context, *Kim Kardashian's Fairytale Wedding* serves to buttress hegemonic norms: gender behavior expectations, definitions of femininity, and what a wedding should look like. The show supports capitalistic ideas of consumerism, that spending money and displaying wealth through expensive gowns, decor, and jewelry signify love. When love is defined through material goods, it cannot last as long as the goods themselves.

CONCLUSION

Keeping Up with the Kardashians exemplifies Turner's (2004) three considerations of celebrity; discourse within the series helps create and sustain celebrity, their celebrity performs social functions (such as assignation of beauty standards and support of materialism) while commodification of their celebrity helps bolster the family's finances as well as permits conspicuous consumption. The televised celebrity ideals are also visible in other media, particularly social media, discussed in the following chapter. However, the flagship television series is the origination point of the Kardashian brand, replete with celebrity, materialism, and sexuality.

Emphases on sexuality and women's conflicted roles are present throughout all the series' dichotomies. The Kardashians normalize body and beauty ideals, which are in part established via television, such as being thin and white (Harrison, 2008; Pozner, 2010). Moreover, they accord with the concept of television's message of transformation being mandatory in order to conform to sexuality and beauty norms (Weber, 2009). This fits their sales messages; buy Kardashian beauty products in order to be beautiful and attain standards (Gill, 2008; McRobbie, 2004).

While their sexual images help define femininity and celebrity, they set unrealistic expectations that even the Kardashians seemingly cannot attain. The lack of attention on the show given to exercise and diet promotes that idea that anyone may attain a seemingly perfect body through surgery and Kardashian products. However, the lack of satisfaction the sisters express about their bodies complicates the strengthening of beauty exemplars; rather, the norm is seemingly constant frustration, a theme with which many viewers likely empathize. While body ideals are vaunted, none of the sisters ever appear content, despite their celebrity and beauty.

Concurrently, while venerating sexual imagery, the Kardashians endorse conservative sexuality norms and are depicted as neither promiscuous nor immoral. Nudity and debauchery are not conjoined on the program. Any negative behavior, such as drunk driving, reaps severe emotional repercussions.

The Kardashian women reinforce female stereotypes, while exploiting them for profit. While other programs also commodify women's sexuality (Lundy, Ruth, & Park, 2008) such as *The Bachelor*, *Rock of Love*, and *The Girls Next Door* (Wood, 2011), *Keeping Up with the Kardashians* differs in one significant way: the Kardashians are knowingly exploiting their own bodies for their own profit, and thus far have tremendously succeeded in this endeavor. Kim and her sisters benefit financially and attain more celebrity by using their bodies and sexuality, contributing to an image based upon sex appeal.

This again ties into conspicuous consumption; the commodified Kardashian image ostensibly requires the maintenance and purchase of Kardashian products, such as the Kardashian-endorsed makeup, fragrances, clothing, and jewelry. The Kardashian celebrity and brand is cyclically engendered by and reliant upon products. The Kardashian audience may be unified through their consumption of the Kardashian brand and celebrity, through purchasing merchandise, watching the shows, and consuming social media. The materialism inherent throughout the Kardashian media is another easily absorbed trait, just like beauty, sisterhood, and sexuality. These simplified ideals amalgamate into an easily packaged, seemingly glamorous, and unending aspirational lifestyle and brand for audiences to consume and imitate.

Chapter Four

Social Media

While televised narratives are clearly visible, narratives are also present, albeit in different forms, throughout social media. In order to ascertain what and how these social media outlets add to the Kardashian brand image, this chapter consists of narrative discourse analyses of Kim Kardashian's blog and Twitter use. The Kardashians chiefly use Facebook to direct traffic to their primary social media outlet, their blogs, and therefore Facebook is not examined in-depth here. As such, the overwhelming majority of the individual family members and the *Keeping Up with the Kardashians* official pages' Facebook posts are links to family members' blogs. Kim, Kourtney, Khloé, and Kris each have their own formal blog, while Kendall and Kylie share one. Social media company Celebuzz, which also hosts Britney Spears and Nicole Ritchie's websites, hosts all of their blogs. Celebuzz is part of Buzzmedia, a company that owns a consortium of popular culture blogs, including gossip sites Just Jared and Pink is the New Blog, music sites Stereogum, Idolater, and Brooklyn Vegan, and the American website for British gossip magazine *OK!*. Buzzmedia also owns the print music magazine *Spin*. They sell advertising across all of their sites, and claim to reach more than 120 million unique visitors per month (Sisaro, 2012).

Family members also make use of other social media as well. For example, Kylie Jenner maintains a fashion-oriented Tumblr blog that consists solely of photographs and animated gifs; an internet-based collage. On Instagram, a photo-sharing social media site owned by Facebook, as of August 2012 several Kardashians ranked in the top ten most popular users: Rob tenth, Kourtney seventh, Kylie fifth, Kendall third, while Kim, with close to four million followers, was the most popular user on the social media outlet (Fitzgerald, 2012). By October of 2012, on Twitter Khloé had close to eight million followers and was the most active celebrity tweeter (Casserly, 2012).

Despite all of the family members' popularity, Kim is by far the most prominent Kardashian social media user.

Kim is intensely popular on Twitter. By September 2012, over sixteen
million users followed her; according to the *New York Times* Kim was the
ninth most influential Twitter user in 2011 (Leonhardt, 2011). As of September 2012, she was the only reality-TV personality within the top twenty most
popular accounts; indeed, the closest ranked reality-TV personality was Ryan
Seacrest, ranked 47th in popularity, who was closely followed by Khloé
Kardashian, rated as 49th (The Twitaholic.com Top 100 Twitterholics based
on Followers, 2012).

This chapter examines narratives within Kim's Twitter feed and her blog.
Narratives throughout all media inform how we understand our world, offline and online. As Chayko (2008) asserts, online stories "provide us with
all-important images with which to populate our sociomental space" (p. 32).
Moreover, "online and mobile technologies help foster our love and need for
narrative" (p. 32). While the study of social media is relatively new, a body
of literature exists that models a number of methodologies. An important
aspect considered is the multimodality of media; media traditionally studied
separately are intertwining, and thus an intertexual perspective is necessary
to study messages being broadcasted and layered through multiple formats.
Indeed, most modern technologies are multimodal, mingling photography,
video, auralities, and the written word (Kress & van Leeuwen, 2006).

Social media research particularly necessitates "observing particular ways
people create and use texts, and investigating the *how* and the *why* of their
text making" (Lee, 2011, p. 113, emphasis in original). There are countless
qualitative methodological approaches to the study of social media. For instance, scholars researching online behavior may conduct in-depth interviews (e.g., Chayko, 2008; Lee, 2011), case studies (e.g., Nip, 2004), or
ethnographies (Kendall, 2002). In addition, some scholars examine the structure of mediated messages, investigating technological, situational, and linguistic variables (e.g., Herring, 1996). In this chapter, the studies primarily
examine Kardashian-constructed messages, and secondarily, fan-constructed
messages. These interactions foster the relationship between the family and
the fan community, help audiences build identities, and function to help form
and bolster the Kardashian brand and celebrity, and thus foster brand loyalty
and profits.

SOCIAL MEDIA AND CELEBRITY

Social media are a relatively recent component added to the arsenal of tools
that construct and sustain celebrity. They are intensely popular; by 2009,
social media "had overtaken porn as the number one activity on the Internet"

(Piazza, 2011, p. 144). Celebrities use social media, such as blogging, Facebook, Twitter, Instagram and the like, to convey messages, augment their mediated identities, and connect with audiences. Social media have the power to greatly raise awareness of a celebrity, perpetuating fame and fortune.

Social media permit an ostensible link between celebrities and audience members. In Schickel's (2000) work on the illusion of intimacy, he contends that relationships between celebrities and audience members do not truly exist. Celebrities perceive a mass audience of undifferentiated individuals. To audience members, the relationship is actually imaginary; he or she does not have a friendship with a celebrity. Social media have the potential to alter the illusion of intimacy, while also perpetuating it. An audience member may feel an even deeper attachment to a celebrity through the celebrity's rendition of mundane facts via social media. However, in opposition to Schickel's ideas, social media permit the famous to directly engage with fans, often opening a dialogue. Through social media people "form real, consequential social bonds with people we have never met face-to-face" (Chayko, 2008, p. 3). Social media facilitate relationships with not only distant friends and family, but also celebrities (Chayko, 2002; 2008). For example, in 2011 a member of the military asked actress Mila Kunis to accompany him to a military ball via YouTube. A female service member created a similar video to invite to Justin Timberlake. Both celebrities attended. In another example, a cancer-stricken teenager asked singer Taylor Swift to his prom through Facebook. The power of social media is such that she was aware of the request and in return, asked him to attend to Academy of Country Music Awards with her (Murray, 2012).

While Brooker (2002) perceives online communication as "structured top-down interactivity," the interactive nature of social media belies this claim. Social media permit unfettered access to "authentic celebrity voice" and may be "privileged channel[s] to the star him/herself" (Muntean & Petersen, 2009). These pathways intensify the relationship between a celebrity and fans (Marshall, 2010). Audience members may comment, ask questions, or otherwise engage with the Kardashians, who often respond to people via Twitter or other media outlets. This interactivity serves to engage consumers; consumers who associate with online entities tend to have higher brand loyalty (Jenkins, 2006).

Furthermore, the fans act as a "focus group," a collective pool of ideas and opinions celebrities may access. When Kim developed her first fragrance, "'She utilized her fans by asking them questions,' says Kecia Coby, brand president of the perfume line. 'Her fans picked the package color, the bottle and the gifting program'" (Newman & Bruce, 2011). The Kardashians utilize their fans/focus groups for many similar types of decisions including the selection of shoe line names and even the title of their fictional novel, *Dollhouse*.

Moreover, all of the Kardashians utilize what Jenkins (1998) termed media convergence, or the marketing of a single product across multiple platforms. This multi-platform interactivity results in cultural convergence, or an online meaning-making process (Jenkins, 1998). Social media engagement between fans and celebrities results in amplified para-social relationships, increased brand loyalty, and a rise in celebrity brand consumption. Given this environment, it is worthwhile to review varied qualitative methodologies and analyses particularly associated with blogs, Facebook, and Twitter.

Blogging

Bloggers are "the Internet's new storytellers" (Lenhart & Fox, 2006). Blogs are "typically expressions of personal or professional opinion or experience on which other people can at most comment" (Vossen & Hagemann, 2007). Blogs may be a personal journal, a tool of promotion, a means of news or information dissemination, or almost any other form of expression.

Blogging and the comments associated with each post provide "rich, complex, and interactional spaces" (Walton & Jaffe, 2011) thus engendering community (Chayko, 2008). Writing a blog also helps build self-identity (Chayko, 2008). Blogs generally contain a set of related links, spurring connectivity and upping visitor traffic.

The amount of blogs is astounding; the total number of blogs doubles every five and a half months (Vossen & Hagemann, 2007, p. 52). According to Technorati, a blog search engine, in 2011 the blogger breakdown consisted of: sixty percent hobbyists (who earn no income from blogging), eighteen percent professional full-time and part-time (who receive compensation for their blogging, but most do not consider it their full time job), thirteen percent entrepreneurs (who blog for their own company or organization), and eight percent corporate (who blog for a company or organization) (Technorati, 2012).

Facebook and Twitter

Facebook is the most dominant social network. Founded in 2004, by October of 2012, Facebook had 1 billion monthly active users (Facebook Newsroom). Almost half of America's population utilizes Facebook (Wasserman, 2012). Like other social networks, it is intended to "help us connect through interactive profiles or pages we design and update" (Chayko, 2008, p. 8). The site "offers its users myriad ways of expressing views, conveying affinities, and establishing connections" (Jones, Schieffelin, & Smith, 2011, p. 27). Facebook, in contrast to top-down media like television, allows multiple methods of communication: "knowledge is presented from many sources, and then ignored and/or negotiated" (Lenihan, 2011, p. 50). Through the ability to comment, "like," and post photos, videos, and links, Facebook and Twitter are becoming increasingly interactive and dialogic (Lee, 2011).

Twitter launched July 15, 2006 (Smith, 2010). By March of 2008, fourteen million people were registered (Ostrow, 2009). According to Twitter.com, as of September 14, 2010 there were "175 million registered users" creating ninety-five million tweets per day (http://twitter.com/about, March 18, 2011). Of course, simply registering for an account doesn't necessarily indicate use. In 2009, at least twenty-seven million users occasionally used Twitter per month. Of those twenty-seven million users, only twenty-seven percent were regular users (Pear Analytics, 2009). By 2012, a Pew Internet report asserted that eight percent of online adults use Twitter daily, a percentage that has quadrupled since 2010 (Smith & Brenner, 2012). Smith and Brenner attribute this rise to the increase of smartphone prevalence. Twitter users may post brief, 140 character messages, called tweets. Twitter and Facebook feature microblogging, "the writing of short messages on the web designed for self-reporting about what one is doing, thinking, or feeling at any moment" (Lee, 2011, p. 111).

Pear Analytics (2009) categorized the contents of tweets thusly: forty percent pointless babble, thirty-eight percent conversational, nine percent self-promotion, four percent spam, and four percent news. Their definition of pointless babble is not clearly elucidated, but seems to be status updates determined as meaningless and mundane, and not directed at anyone in particular, i.e.; "I ate a turkey sandwich for lunch."

Those most likely to use Twitter include people age eighteen to twenty, African-Americans, and urbanites. Of people using the site, about half are between the ages of eighteen and thirty-four (Dugan, 2011). Women and college-educated people are slightly more likely to use the site. Moreover, twenty-five percent of users visit the site multiple times per day. People typically post updates about their personal lives or jobs, resend others' tweets, and/or note where they currently are.

As Twitter has grown in popularity, the academic world has taken notice. A number of authors have considered the potential of Twitter as a tool for journalists (for example, Ahmad, 2010; Carmicheal, 2009; Farhi, 2009), others examined the role Twitter played in the Iranian (Morozov, 2009), Moldovan (Mungiu-Pippidi and Munteanu, 2009), and Egyptian uprisings (Papacharissi & de Fatima Oliveira, 2012), and more study how it is used in varied fields, such as environmentalism (Clark, 2009; Marshall, Stuart, and Jaunzens, 2010) and medicine (Cain, Scott, and Smith, 2010; Greysen, Kind, and Chretien, 2010; Hawn, 2009). Additionally, scholars have explored Twitter's use in public relations (Gilpin, 2011; Xifra and Grau, 2010). In Gilpin's (2011) study, she examined how public relations practitioners utilize Twitter to develop professional personas. Napoli (2010) importantly noted that Twitter, as well as other user-generated media outlets such as YouTube and

Facebook, situates average users as equal to "traditional institutional communicators" (p. 509).

Marwick and boyd (2010) appraised the strategies Twitter users employ to reach particular audiences. Using Goffman's (1959) notion of impression management, they aver that Twitter reflexively requires a user and an audience to formulate the user's identity. Social media "collapse diverse social contexts into one" making construction and negotiation of authenticity contextual upon audiences (Marwick and boyd, 2010, p. 10). Marwick and boyd assert two means are used to mitigate Twitter authenticity tensions: "self-censorship and balance." Self-censorship refers to omission of certain subjects, while balance refers to countering strategic tweets with more personal messages.

In regard to celebrity Twitter use, Marshall (2010) explored how stars utilize Twitter and Facebook to fashion their own adaption of Goffman's (1959) idea of self-presentation. On these social networks, celebrities conflate their personal and professional lives, creating a version of themselves for public consumption. The sundry and linked social network platforms are the new public stage, resulting in three levels of "the public version of the private self" (Marshall, 2010, p. 44). The first level, the public self, consists of a purely professional manner of conduct within social media, possibly maintained by celebrity intermediaries, such as managers; the second, the public private self, is the acknowledgment of a private self through participation in social media. The third level, the transgressive intimate self, is related to Hill's (2007) moments of authenticity; the genuine self is visible through instances where undeniably true emotion is transmitted.

Marwick and boyd (2011) also reference Goffman's (1959) work in their examination of celebrity as performative practice on Twitter. They find that through Twitter, celebrities offer a seemingly candid glimpse into "backstage," or their real lives. Indeed, celebrity tweeting is "equated with the assertion of the authentic celebrity voice" and often used to "counter ersatz narratives" (Muntean and Petersen, 2009). The celebrities in Marwick and boyd's (2011) study, Mariah Carey, Perez Hilton, and Miley Cyrus, "performed intimacy, affiliation, and public acknowledgment" actions on Twitter. These behaviors help establish the Twitter audience as fans and in turn, help reify celebrity status. Marwick and boyd cite public recognition and fan maintenance (recognition of a fan community), affiliation (public connection between celebrity and fans), and intimacy (para-social interaction resulting in familiarity) as methods of nourishing fame through Twitter. As noted later, Kim Kardashian employs these methods in addition to broadcasting overtly financially-driven tweets.

Kim Kardashian's Twitter account is a "verified celebrity" account; it truly is her issuing the tweets. While many celebrities have an assistant or manager wielding his or her account, Kardashian's linguistic style indicates that she is actually typing or texting tweets. This voice is valuable to brands. A *Hollywood Reporter* article asserted that Kardashian,

> charges as much as $25,000 to simply mention and link to a brand or company in a tweet. It's so effective a tool that businesses have begun including Twitter clauses in their contracts with the family, committing the girls to a set number of tweets about their product (Newman & Bruce, 2011).

For example, a single 2010 tweet issued by Kim publicizing Armani drove 40,000 users to the Armani website within 24 hours (Shepatin, 2010). In 2010, Kim had only had 2.7 million Twitter followers; as of September 2012 she had over 16 million. The company Ad.ly, a "social-media advertorial clearinghouse [that] pairs brands with celebs to inject highly personalized advertising into their Twitter streams" lists Kim as their top performing tweeter (Piazza, 2012).

The Kardashians utilize many forms of social media. For instance, Kim Kardashian's smart phone app costs $1.99 and includes lifestyle and fashion tips, her constantly updated Twitter stream, and a weekly question and answer session. A user can also interact with an animated version of Kim. The *Keeping Up with the Kardashians* smart phone app features updated Twitter streams from family members, news, games, and photo and video galleries. It is free; it promotes engagement, community membership, and brand loyalty.

THE NEW CELEBRITY: KIM KARDASHIAN AND SOCIAL MEDIA

Marwick and boyd (2010) maintain that Twitter performs in a variety of ways: "as a broadcast medium, marketing channel, diary, social platform, and news source" (p. 9). Kim utilizes all of these functions, building her celebrity, audience, and brand. This chapter examines how social media, like Twitter, permits celebrities such as Kim Kardashian to sustain fame and fortune by building a portrayal of authenticity while simultaneously intensely self-promoting. As Kim herself noted, "I really do believe I am a brand for my fans" (Wilson, 2010).

Daniel Boorstin famously labeled a celebrity as someone who is known for his well-knownness (1961/1992). Boorstin was prescient. Over time, celebrities transformed from aviator and military heroes, to high-aura movie stars (Langer, 1981), to familiar TV actors (Marshall, 1997), to today's self-promoting reality TV participants. Many of these new celebrities are savvy at promoting themselves through social media. Here, I explore the contemporary interaction of celebrity and social media through analysis of Kim Kardashian's avid use of Twitter, and subsequently, her blog. Twitter, a social network gaining in popularity, is important to study within the context of celebrity in order to understand how new media is affecting society. This study of Kim Kardashian's Twitter interactions can be extrapolated to any future social network that may develop. This investigation reveals not only the sociocultural significance of Twitter but also the sociocultural significance of celebrity culture.

The Kardashians realize that the show helps build a fan base, which is then nurtured through social media (Wilson, 2010). However, social media permits more than simply building and maintaining a fan base. Through Twitter and her blog, Kim is able to refine an authentic persona. She reveals to fans a constructed "behind-the-scenes" glimpse of the "real" person behind the celebrity façade. She broadcasts where she is and what she's doing, posts self-taken photos of herself and her friends, interacts with fans, and is seemingly candid about inconsequential aspects of her life. Particularly on the egalitarian Twitter, Kim's fans superficially enjoy equal communication opportunities as her celebrity friends. Kim's use of Twitter positions her as equal to everyone else able to utilize the service, modifying her celebrity status. Concurrently, some of the content of her tweets validates her celebrity status.

On Twitter, the audience for Kim Kardashian actively works, engaging with her, reading her tweets, retweeting, and sometimes replying to her. Social media and Twitter in particular reconfigure the cultural studies conception of the active audience into a literal one. Following Jenkins (2006) contention that online audience activity promotes brand loyalty, Kim's Twitter followers may be understood as a devoted audience, more likely to purchase her perfume, visit her stores, and watch her shows. This resonates with the concept that "communication itself also becomes a revenue generator for [web 2.0] media organizations" (Napoli, 2010, p. 512). Arguments along these lines often focus on data mining and online advertisements geared toward users specific preferences or integrated into their own pages (for example, Andrejevic, 2011; Cohen, 2008; Deuze, 2007; Spurgeon, 2008). While a Twitter follower of Kim may spread "word of mouth" awareness and promote the Kim Kardashian brand through retweets and mentions, this consumer is even more engaged by being able to communicate directly with Kim herself. This exemplifies and extends what Napoli terms new media's "content production/distribution/exhibition/consumption dynamic" (2010, p. 513). Kim's use of Twitter engenders the possibility of an extremely active and engaged audience. This audience member/producer/consumer does more than simply consume, voluntarily becoming a creator and adding content, promotion, and importantly endorsement, helping to construct Kim's brand.

Many authors interrogate the blurred boundary between online audiences' participation and exploitation (for example, Andrejevic, 2011; Arvidsson, 2007; Banks and Humphreys, 2008). From a Marxist perspective, Andrejevic (2011) contends that online audiences create value for others through enjoyed, yet free labor. Certainly this is true of Kim's Twitter followers as well.

As previously noted, Kim herself declared that "Twitter is the most amazing focus group out there" (Wilson, 2010). Newman and Bruce (2011) noted Kim engages her followers in "the decision-making process surrounding . . . endorsements, empowering them with a sense of ownership." Kim affirmed, "Many of our ideas [about what to endorse] come from our fans and then our mother makes it happen" (Newman and Bruce, 2011).

Her Twitter feed is a supplement to the personality shown on *Keeping Up with the Kardashians* and shows of its ilk. There is one essential difference between television and Twitter: the camera eventually turns off. Kim on Twitter does not. Fans follow her in real time, staying up-to-date through her constant posting. As intimate as television may be, it is recorded months in advance. Twitter is now. Her timely Twitter stream adds to her authenticity construction, reifies her celebrity status, and helps capitalize her brand.

As Jeff Jensen stated in a September 2010 *Entertainment Weekly* article, Kim is a "mad tweeter with 4.5 million followers" (p. 46). Followers are Twitter users who choose to automatically receive Kim's Twitter updates. By November 2010, over 5.3 million followed her (Wilson, 2010). By March 2011, over 6.9 million people followed Kim. In November 2011, almost 11 million users followed her. Finally, as noted earlier, as of September of 2012, more than 16 million people followed her.

Importantly, Kim has an "ability to direct web traffic" (O'Dell, 2010). Her website receives 40 million hits per month with 20 percent of the traffic coming from Twitter feed click-throughs (Newman and Bruce, 2011). On Twitter, Kim is the celebrity user with the most click-throughs; people reading her tweets are likely to click on a web link she posts, which most frequently leads to her blog (O'Dell, 2010). Her official blog, the most visited of any celebrity, is only outranked in popularity by sports, news, and media hosting sites (such as Flickr and Vimeo). As O'Dell noted "In short, Kardashian's [Twitter] stream is optimized to gracefully direct traffic to her website. And her website is optimized for the social web, too, with tweets and blog posts prominently featured" (2010).

Kim's tweets are a unique blend of commercial and personal. As O'Dell noted, Kim,

> tweets personable, relatable clickbait. Fans are alerted about pictures of her European outfits, a contest to attend her birthday party, a breast cancer awareness drive—the kind of content her fans clearly want to see. The rest of her tweets are social; such a statement seems obvious until you scan other streams that reek of PR and marketing influence, begging followers to buy a product or consume content. Other celeb streams are almost entirely link-free and designed to facilitate interaction around that individual's personality rather than create a desired action in the user. (2010, p.1)

Kim simultaneously builds her authenticity, celebrity stature, and brand through real-time updates and interaction. Through a narrative analysis, this study analyzes Kim's Twitter and blog utilization, exploring how celebrity, new media, and commerce intertwine.

For this initial portion of this study, I examined three months of Kim's tweets. From January 1, 2011 to March 31, 2011, Kim Kardashian generated 921 tweets. Her tweets included status updates, replies, and retweets. Anything she posted was included in this study. After reading the entire tweet set, I classified each into one of six narratives based upon thematic content. This time period was chosen as representative of the year 2011; the following analysis of her blog takes place during 2012.

From January 1, 2011 to March 31, 2011, Kim averaged 10.23 tweets per day. Kim generally tweeted within six narratives explored here: personal tidbits, lifestyle, interaction with fans, interaction with celebrities, encouraging traffic to website, and promotional/publicity. Reality television is at the "forefront of the convergence of broadcast television and networking technologies" (Butler, 2006, p. 119). Many television programs incorporate aspects of social media; the Kardashians use it to enhance their celebrity and brand. As such, an integral component of reality-TV-formulated celebrity is social media.

Personal Tidbits

Kim builds celebrity in two ways on Twitter; creating/reassuring fans of her likable normality and displaying her glamorous celebrity lifestyle. One way she accomplishes this is through personal tidbit tweets. Gamson (1994) states the celebrity tidbit is a valuable piece of information, used to create publicity in media. In social media format, while Kim does use these to generate some publicity, her personal facts and musings primarily help create authenticity. Building authenticity is integral to being liked and thus aids in earning fame. Through the personal tidbit, fans are seemingly permitted some insight into Kim's state of mind, her daily life, and her personality. Of course, these are aspects of her life that she chooses to share.

Many tidbits establish her normality. Fans may be able to relate to her through her seemingly ordinariness. She complains, "I'm soooo sleepy, too lazy to get up and wash my make up off and brush my teeth but I need to! Help" (January 30, 2011). She has cravings, claiming "Nothing better than a little late night cookies n cream ice cream!" (January 30, 2011) and "I am addicted to french fries! #help" (March 10, 2011).

She's average in other ways: "Going to bed early . . . good night, tweet dreams!" (March 03, 2011) and "Good morning! Heading to church with the family then Sunday brunch! Hope you all have a relaxing day today!" (March 06, 2011).

Throughout the day, Kim might let fans know facts through tweets like these: "Kim fact-I hate pepper and peppers!" (January 06, 2011), "I feel out of the loop when I'm out of town! I can't wait to see my sisters today!" (January 05, 2011), "The word chillax annoys me on another level!" (January 09, 2011), "Elizabeth Taylor and Sofia Loren are my ultimate idols!" (January 11, 2011), "Fun fact-The guy that was in Katy Perry's Teenage Dream video was also the guy in my Skechers commercial" (February 13, 2011), or "I really want a salt water aquarium. My dream is to have some sea horses! They are just soooo cute!" (March 12, 2011).

Kim alerts her fans to where she is and what she's doing, for example, tweeting "I love LA! Such a hot sunny day! Big change from NY freezing weather! Love mixing it up!" (January 24, 2011) and "Eating lunch w my sisters, masey, and friends! Couldn't be yummier and happier!" (January 28, 2011).

Emotions help convey authenticity for reality TV participants (McClain, 2011). Kim includes emotions within her Twitter stream of fun facts and personality insights. She tweeted, "I just drove for the 1st time in NYC! Got a little scared driving over a bridge, I'm afraid of heights . . . but the tunnel was cool!" (March 09, 2011). In a seemingly sincere tone, she expressed, "I miss my Valentine :-(" (February 14, 2011) and "I miss my humpkin" (February 25, 2011). A keen fan might know her current boyfriend was NBA star Kris Humphries, whom she nicknamed Humpkin. This bit of insider knowledge privileges the ardent fan. Another day, Kim posted a photo along with this tweet: "Happy Birthday Dad! Celebrating at his favorite Armenian restaurant w the family! http://twitpic.com/42sgka" (February 22, 2011). While seemingly innocuous, almost any casual fan or viewer of her programs realizes that Kim's father died several years ago. This seemingly happy update is her family's annual remembrance celebration.

Numerous personal tidbit tweets are vague and apparently trite. However, many are directed at devoted fans, who understand the context and importance of certain tweets. Thus, the tweets cultivate fandom, engaging contextual knowledge and encouraging a feeling of a direct link with Kim. Moreover, the banal tweets listing her work, locations, and actions provide at least of modicum of superficial knowledge about her everyday life, while her emotions provide sincerity. All of these factors collude in constructing Kim's overall authenticity.

Lifestyle

Tweets about her glamorous, yet real life are similar to personal tidbits. These emphasize her thrilling lifestyle and highlight work as well. This amalgamation of traits establishes that her celebrity existence is fabulous, but earned. Fans glimpse a lifestyle abounding in high-end fashion, glam-squad make-overs, and exciting photo shoots. The lifestyle tweets substantiate that Kim is undeniably a celebrity and justifies this distinction.

Kim demonstrated her glamorous life, saying "Oscar day madness has begun! About to start glamming up! I have my J Mendel dress with Lorraine Schwartz jewels! Think blue! twit pic soon" (February 27, 2011). She included a picture with this tweet: "Almost ready for the Grammy's! Fun glam day with @EvaLongoria http://twitpic.com/3zidne" (February 13, 2011).

Her tweets express that she completes difficult work, earning her glamorous lifestyle. Kim complained, "I can't believe it's 4:30am and I'm up for a full press day! #sleepy" (January 19, 2011) and "Rise and grind! Family meeting today! We are working on a fun new project all together! Love when we all work together!" (February 17, 2011). Kim also tweeted about her thrilling lifestyle, "I left the Golden Globes party and came home to a midnight spray tan! LOL . . . Thanks Jimmy CoCo for the late nite tan!" (January 17, 2011).

A common tweet is the cheerful "Rise and Grind!!!!" or "Rise and grind! Gym time!!!" (January 27, 2011). Kim frequently utilizes this greeting to begin her day of tweets. She is awake; she is working.

Many of her tweets are about exercising. As someone who is known for her shapely figure, these tweets help justify her body-based celebrity: "So glad I woke up early and went to bootcamp! Early morning workouts just make my day better!" (January 25, 2011), "I tried a new workout today and I loved it! #Beastmode" (February 28, 2011), and "Whats up world? I had another hard workout today . . . I am sooo sore, I can't even move!" (March 03, 2011).

Kim shares television appearances, particularly noting her high-end fashion choices. She updated her fans: "Just did Regis and Kelly! Loving my pale pink @ZacPosen dress . . . no time to change, back to the Today Show w Kathie Lee and Hoda!" (January 19, 2012). Later that day, she continued "About to do @PiersMorgan's new show with my sister @KourtneyKardash! I love him, so excited for this!" (January 19, 2011). She often includes pictures, enticing her fans with literal glimpses into her day's thrilling work. These tweets included photograph links: "GLAMAZON! Love my glam team @GlamSquadBTS aka Joyce Bonelli and Frankie Payne! http://twitpic.com/3tffhh" (January 25, 2011), "On set in my Midori green dress! http://twitpic.com/3tfgyo" (January 25, 2011), and "Loving my Glamour mag cover!!! http://bit.ly/hXwMmm Such a fun and flirty shoot!" (January 03, 2011).

Fan Interaction

Twitter provides fans an opportunity to directly interact with Kim. She jokes with them, asks and answers questions, and encourages her fan community. Moreover, she often thanks fans. This communication rewards followers and at the same time makes her seem grateful. She appears sincere, normal, and thankful for her popularity.

Kim often directly answers questions and dispels rumors. Responding to a tweet, she wrote "Yes! We do it every year! RT @iheartkimnet @KimKardashian is your family tradition to wear the same pajamas on Christmas Day? :)" (January 07, 2011) and "No, just a rumor! I hope to one day though! RT @stefidragoi @KimKardashian I heard that you are coming to Austria in February" (January 15, 2011).

She thanks fans, concurrently promoting her shows through fan adoration: "Thanks for watching! RT @Josh4Thompson This show is awesome! I'm so glad its finally on TV! @KourtneyKardash @KimKardashian can I get a RT?" (January 23, 2011) and "thx doll RT @MHallak0426 @KimKardashian I've only watch 15 minutes of Kourtney and Kim Take New York and I OFCOURSE already LOVE it (: <333" (January 24, 2011). Using the endearment "doll" affirms her supposed friendship with the fan. Kim also nurtures her fan community. On January 24, 2011, she exclaimed, "OMG I just reached 6 million followers! You guys are everything to me! I love and appreciate you! LOVE MY TWIT FAM! Xoxo." A few days later, she excitedly noted (and helpfully provided a link) "OMG!! I just passed 4 million 'likes' on Facebook!! http://on.fb.me/kimfbook Thank u guys, I love u all! Xo" (January 28, 2011). Similarly, she appreciated other online fans, saying "Shout out to all of my KimKardashian.com friends. I've been reading all of your comments on my blog posts! I LOVE U GUYS! Xoxo" (March 11, 2011).

Lastly, Kim polls fans for personal-life suggestions. This makes her seem ordinary. Followers may interact with her as they would with anyone else. She asked, "I need new music for my ipod! Suggestions?" (February 15, 2011) and even "Anyone know any remedies for psoriasis?" (February 28, 2011).

Celebrity Interaction

Kim's visible interaction with other celebrities online also constructs fame. Fans can marvel at her friendships with other stars. This also lends to the overall authenticity and credibility of her Twitter stream. In these interactions Kim is seemingly interacting with her true friends; presumably she wouldn't present them with a false persona.

On January 14, 2011, she tweeted "OMG @JustinBieber just stopped by to give us tickets to his movie Never Say Never! http://twitpic.com/3q24ll" and included a picture of Justin Bieber with her and her sisters.

Likewise, she included pictures of herself with *Glee* star Chris Colfer (with him holding his newly-won Golden Globe), Chaka Khan and Kelly Osbourne, and Heidi Klum. In another example, Kim communicated with the infamous Lindsay Lohan and reality TV star Snooki. Kim responded to Lindsay "Love u! Let's take NY! RT @lindsaylohan Can't wait for @KimKardashian and @KourtneyKardash Take NYC! My home town! Love you girls! Xoxo" (January 22, 2011). She responded similarly to Snooki, "Love u snookaroo! Hang out in Jerz soon! RT @Sn00ki: @JonathanCheban @KimKardashian So nice to see you guys tonight! Love you bitches! Xoxo" (January 22, 2011). Kim also welcomed another ostensible friend to Twitter: "OMG I'm so excited Christina Aguilera just joined twitter!!! Please give a warm twitter welcome to my girl @TheRealXtina FOLLOW HER! Xo" (March 22, 2011).

Kim also often converses with well-known friends on Twitter. She asked "Girls dinner tonight @lala @ciara @BrittGastineau @serenawilliams???" (March 15, 2011). Lala is former MTV VJ and reality TV participant La La Vazquez, Ciara is a prominent hip-hop musician, Brittny Gastineau is another reality TV performer, and Serena Williams is a professional tennis player. Later that month, Kim reached out to Serena, "Read ur bbm! calling u RT @serenawilliams: @KimKardashian @KELLYROWLAND @lala I really need help #whatshisname has me near tears I ruined it" (March 20, 2011). Kim apparently has genuine relationships with these public figures. Broadcasting these friendships performs varied functions: followers can feel as if they're a part of these friendships; they view Kim sincerely interacting with her friends, and other celebrities help warrant Kim's fame. After all, if Kim socializes with these celebrities, this puts her at the same rarified status. Not everyone is able to attend Golden Globe parties, meet Chaka Khan, and comfort Serena Williams.

Prominent people also validate Kim's renown, frequently complimenting her. Of course, by doing this on Twitter they also reach Kim's millions of followers. Haute couture designer Vera Wang (or the person who tweets for her) complimented Kardashian, in a tweet that Kardashian resent to her followers: "So much fun RT @VeraWangGang Great hanging w @KimKardashian @Rachel_Roy & @JonathanCheban 2night. Super chic people that always look fabulous" (January 23, 2011). Former Destiny's Child singer Kelly Rowland and singer Ciara recommended that people watch Kardashian's new show, tweets Kim replied to, saying "Love u guys!!!! RT @KELLYROWLAND RT @ciara: Check out my girl @KimKardashian show tonight as well. Kourtney Kim Take New York! Go Girls!" (January 23, 2011). Likewise, Kim responded to *Jersey Shore* reality TV star Pauly D's recommendation of her new single, saying "Thanks Pauly RT @DJPaulyD I Think @KimKardashian Is Talking To Me In Her New Track She Says 'Turn It Up' 'Turn It Up'!!! Dope Track Girl" (March 2, 2011).

Traffic Tweets

As previously noted, Kim's Twitter feed guides traffic to her blog. In fact, one of every five of her website visitors comes from a Twitter link (O'Dell, 2010). Kim typically encourages fans to visit her blog by linking to new pictures or information on her site.

Examples of tweets that push visitors to her site include these: "Exciting news about our Kardashian Kollection! http://bit.ly/dHSLuc" (January 12, 2011) and "Special message to my young twitter fam! http://bit.ly/g0oKTM" (January 19, 2011). In today's media-saturated world, the promise of new information lures people to her site.

Likewise, posting new images on her site can entice fans. These tweets alert followers there is a new photo for them to see: "Playing dress up with Mason! http://bit.ly/dFPwYq" (February 21, 2011), "How do @kourtneykar-dash and I look as cartoons?? http://bit.ly/eiidGU" (January 27, 2011), and "Pics from my last day in the recording studio! http://bit.ly/fELc28 I'm gon-na share some pics from my music vid tomorrow morn on my blog!" (March 01, 2011).

Similarly, she tempted followers by mentioning another minor celebrity and promising more pictures, "OMG! Look what @nicolerichie and I found!! http://bit.ly/ePTM2m I screamed when I saw this!" (March 09, 2011) and "A look back at my magazine covers . . . http://bit.ly/ex2ZWG" (March 10, 2011). By inducing fans to visit her site, she persistently increases her publicity and the number of site visitors.

Promotional Tweets

Kim uses Twitter to promote several products: goods she is hired to endorse, her family's various TV shows, and her own merchandise.

She is a paid spokesperson for QuickTrim, a diet supplement. Twice monthly, she posted advertising tweets like these: "Need to lose those holi-day pounds? Enter QuickTrim's Lose To Win's Contest! Buy QuickTrim and sign up now" (January 3, 2011) and "QuickTrim's such a success! If it's helped u lose weight too, register @ quicktrimcontest.com 4 a chance 2 win $50k & be a QT spokesperson!" (January 25, 2011). These ads are written in Kim's voice, yet are clearly paid for by QuickTrim. Unsuspecting consu-mers, possibly young fans, might not realize these are advertisements.

Similarly, Kim tweeted about Skechers shoes, "Enter my sweepstakes for a chance to win a workout with me, $500 shopping spree, and get fifteen percent off Shape-ups! http://on.fb.me/breakup2shapeup" (February 25, 2011), "Here are the #Shapeups I wore on the set of my @skechersusa shoot this week! http://bit.ly/dSjXhU" (January 08, 2011) and "I'm #BreakingUp-

With my trainer because I only need Shape-ups. Let me know what you're #BreakingUpWith" (February 16, 2011).

Helpfully providing links for online shopping, Kim also shilled for other products: "I love @couturepops line of apparel. It's perfect 4 any candy girl. Check out the I Want Candy sweater- 1 of my favs! www.sugarfactory.com" (January 05, 2011), "So excited to be the new face of Midori! Loving the Super Sour cocktail! http://on.fb.me/gTgIVH @drinkmidori http://twit-pic.com/45fh8z" (March 02, 2011) and "just found the site with the best 1-day deals, LivingSocial . . . check 'em out -> http://jol.ly/0n1I RT if you love a great deal. #ad" (January 19, 2011). This last tweet, for Living Social, is clearly marked as an advertisement. However, ads are only sporadically labeled.

Kim also promotes her own shows and products. When *Kourtney and Kim Take New York* aired, she hyped it all day: "With @KourtneyKardash doing Kourtney and Kim Take New York press all day! Can't wait for u guys to see it!" (January 10, 2011), "I'm so excited that Kourtney & Kim Take New York premieres tonight!!! I hope u all tune in tonight, lets live tweet during the 1st episode!" (January 23, 2011), and "Kourtney and Kim Takes New York starts in 10mins East Coast! Can't wait!" (January 30, 2011). She also linked to her own press coverage and advertisements. She tweeted, "Follow @JasonBinn the man on the move! @KourtneyKardash & I are loving NYC, read about it in @gothammag http://tinyurl.com/494pt54" (January 27, 2011) and "OMG! Look at my Times Square billboard! http://bit.ly/gQTYRe" (January 21, 2011).

She promoted her DASH clothing stores, clothing lines, and fragrances several times throughout the three month study: "I love surprising the Dash Dolls at Dash NYC! OMG such cute stuff!" (January 21, 2011), "We have so many new K-Dash items to show you on @QVC tonight, like this: http://bit.ly/eGUSSl 9pm ET, tune in!" (February 25, 2011) and "As a special gift to you guys, right now you can get 25% off my fragrance by entering the promo code DASH at checkout. http://bit.ly/exzge5" (March 03, 2011). Kim used a fan to promote her fragrance, retweeting and commenting, "Haha Love! RT @_ASHJ Just saw a huge @KimKardashian fragrance 18 wheeler ad.! Best ad I've seen in a long time! :) http://twitpic.com/3navq1" (January 05, 2011).

In early March, Kim made her singing debut, embarking into a new component of the entertainment industry. Accordingly, she utilized Twitter to direct attention to her new single "Jam," exclaiming "This was just a fun new experience! I am so glad I went for it! And the proceeds to JAM are being donated to St. Judes Children's hospital" (March 02, 2011). She continued, "OMG I can't sleep! I premiere my song JAM tomorrow w Ryan Seacrest! It hits itunes tomorrow too! I can't wait for you guys to hear it!!!!" (March 02, 2011) and "My song, Jam, is available on iTunes! http://bit.ly/

dPwt01 50% of proceeds will go to St Jude Children's Research Hospital! @MrTeriusNash" (March 02, 2011).

Finally, Kim uses her followers as focus groups, asking for their participation. She tweeted, "We are naming our styles of shoes for Sears . . . should we name them after US cities? Any ideas?" (March 05, 2011) and "Ok now heading to a fragrance meeting. I need a name for my new perfume! Any cool ideas?" (March 23, 2011). Involving her fans mines their creativity and involves them in her products. Online engagement helps link users' identities to brand characteristics (McClain, 2010) and helps promote brand loyalty (Jenkins, 2006). Kardashian also gets her fans involved early, building anticipation for new ventures. She noted in January, "Had a great clothing meeting w my sisters about our Sears line! Its looking so good, can't wait!" (January 31, 2011).

DISCUSSION

Kim's Twitter use exemplifies the new face of celebrity. By actively embracing social media to detail the minutia of her life, Kim constructs a persona with a number of dualities: ordinary/extraordinary, likable/famous, and authentic/glamorous. She employs social media to achieve this construction through fan interaction, establishing her normality and legitimizing her celebrity. Kim's embrace of social media typifies the revised expectation of the fan/celebrity relationship. Today, a celebrity is often minimally expected to interact with fans through new media. Kim is an ideal model of how social media help support older media in creating and sustaining celebrity. If Twitter and blogs had existed previous to 2006, perhaps other celebrities would have outlasted their fifteen minutes.

Online media presents a somewhat different version of Kim than on television. Television is edited to preserve plots, fit time constraints, and to present certain personality characteristics. Twitter is casual, immediate, and interactive, presenting a more realistic version of Kim. Twitter minimizes the ability to refine and edit. Television is inherently a visual medium; Twitter a mobile, text-based medium. Without Kim's face and body, her words take on more significance.

Tweets amplify Kim's celebrity, permitting an "inside" look at her glamorous lifestyle. In the lifestyle and celebrity interaction tweets, Kim affirms her celebrity through celebrity relationships, affinity for high-end clothing, and displaying a glamorous lifestyle. She also details her work, justifying her fame. This results in Marwick and boyd's (2010) concept of "balance," offsetting her promotional, clearly business-motivated tweets with ostensibly personal, if banal, revelations. However, many superficially prosaic tweets are directed to fervent fans, who may detect more intimate meanings through contextual knowledge.

Moreover, Kim's tweets fit nicely into Marshall's (2010) tri-level conception of persona displays. Her promotional and traffic tweets are the public self, presented for consumption without commentary. Her public-private level is perceptible through trivial tweets, for example, messages about food preference or location. These tweets reveal very little about Kim's inner personality. Marshall's third level, the transgressive intimate self, is complex. Judging emotional sincerity on a static, text-based medium such as Twitter, even in conjunction with some self-provided photos, is problematic. However, as noted earlier, some tweets do seem to convey emotions, exposing Kim's "intimate self." At least, as much of her intimate self as she chooses to divulge.

New media is more than simply an extension of old media. Through Twitter, Kim is able to interact individually with fans, using their communication to promote her own interests. She cultivates these fan relationships, encouraging followers to venerate and approve her celebrity through fandom, and also to further her economic interests. This matches Marwick and boyd's (2011) notion of intimacy as a celebrity Twitter practice, with the added component of monetarily-driven tweets.

Two of the six tweet narratives are explicitly financial. The traffic tweets elevate Kim's celebrity, pushing her to the top of traffic-related lists of online celebrity. Additionally, the promotional tweets serve dual functions. On one level, they simply urge followers to buy QuickTrim or watch *Kourtney and Kim Take New York*. On another level, the promotional tweets engage followers, asking for their participation. In this sense Twitter *is* a focus group, allowing followers to seemingly have agency. Concurrently, this helps build loyalty to Kim and her products. If followers interact positively with Kim, they are more likely to consume her cultural and physical products. These tweets are more than just commercials.

Several of Kim's tweets could be placed into two or more categories. A tweet about her show airing that night is a promotional device and also may exhibit sincere excitement. Kim the brand and Kim the real person are successfully fused. She is able to promote products because of her authentic image, likable presentation, and celebrity. She is alternately high-status and a real person; combining celebrity (photo-shoots, celebrity friendships) with real-world sensibilities (fun facts, fan interactions, emotions). Kim Kardashian embodies the intersection of two different online worlds: the seemingly pointless babble of status updates constructing her celebrity/authenticity and the commercialism of online consumerism and advertising. Through Twitter, Kim simultaneously is "real," a celebrity, and a promotional tool. Twitter and social media in general permit a comprehensive and immediate identity construction and deeper loyalty to and expansion of a branding empire.

Throughout all six tweets narratives, the fans willingly engage with Kim. They retweet her updates, reply directly to her, and solicit her attention, sometimes begging her to retweet their posts. The attentive audience, huge in number and ardent in interaction, is part of her brand. Hiring Kim includes acquiring their eyes, minds, and buying power. Social media like Twitter makes their presence highly visible and their eagerness doubtlessly attracts business. Moreover, Twitter facilitates the type of consumer evident through this study; rabidly communicative, intensely loyal, and more than active or interactive. The Twitter fans are actually a part of Kim's brand, collaborating with her, and advocating for and promoting her brand. They are more than simply a mass audience; each is an individual consumer/producer/distributor/ endorser, approving her product ventures, and working in tandem with Kim to bolster her celebrity, brand, and economic interests.

KIM KARDASHIAN'S BLOG

Kim has the highest-ranked individual celebrity blog in terms of unique visitors (O'Dell, 2010); her site receives 40 million hits per month (Newman and Bruce, 2011). The second portion of this study follows the same format as the Twitter study; a comprehensive narrative analysis of three months of Kim's blog, from June 1, 2012, to August 31, 2012.

Kim's blog, located at http://kimkardashian.celebuzz.com, consists primarily of a series of posts listed in chronological order, with the most recent nearest the top of the page. These left-aligned posts take up approximately two-thirds of the page width, while the right-hand third contains buttons to like Kim on Facebook, to follow her on Twitter, and to sign up for her RSS feed (receiving notification when a new blog entry is posted). Below the social media buttons are links to family members' blogs, recent videos posted by Kim, and celebuzz top stories. Under those links are advertisements, including ads for ShoeDazzle, Kim's fragrances, the Sears Kardashian Kollection, and *Keeping Up with the Kardashians*. The top portion of the blog provides links to five selections: home, photos, videos, store, bio, and press. Photos, videos, and press are groupings of blog entries, while the store section solicits users to join the website by providing personal information, while devoid of any actual items available for purchase.

During the three months of this study, the blog contained an average of 3.4 posts per day, and in total, 316 blog entries. The blog posts are primarily about fashion; almost every post includes a photo (typically of Kim), and often only one line of description. She usually appears glamorous and with perfectly prepared makeup and hair. Her longer posts characteristically begin with a greeting directed to her fans, whom she calls dolls, and ends with XO, the symbol for hug and kiss. These intimate salutations foster community and para-social relationships. Indeed, community is an ongoing theme throughout the seven narratives discovered via the narrative analysis, as is materialism. This analysis finds seven blog posting classifications, each contributing to a significant narrative: family and authenticity, celebrity, business, behind the scenes, beauty, social media, and an amalgamated category of family/business/celebrity.

Family and Authenticity

A principal narrative evident throughout the analysis is family and authenticity. When taken superficially as a whole, these blog posts construct a narrative of a young woman close to her family, prone to posting snapshots of them and discussing how much she misses them at a given moment. This narrative also works to position Kim as a "real" person, participating in activities like any normal person, namely spending time with family and friends. A real-time component adds to Kim's authenticity; many of these posts are listed as being "From Kim's Phone" implying that she takes the picture herself, and uploads it to the blog within minutes. This instantaneous nature facilitates a feeling of immediacy and of direct communication with Kim.

One method Kim uses to generate authenticity is by posting old family photos and pictures of herself as a child. For instance, she posted a photo of herself as a child that hangs on a wall in her Grandmother's store (June 4, 2012). Similarly, a week later she posted a photo of Bruce as a child, as well as a photo of Bruce and Kris as a young couple (June 14, 2012). Youthful photos of her and varied family members are a staple of the blog.

Many posts, usually depict casual moments of Kim and her family engaged in various activities: eating lunch with Rob and Khloé, visiting the San Diego Zoo, or celebrating birthdays together. These posts have titles like "Sisterly Love," "Family BBQ!," "Family & Fireworks," "Family Fun In Mexico," "Dinner With The Family In SD," etc.

There are also numerous photos of her nephew, Mason, with blog posts titles like "I Love Him," "Silly Time!" and "Movie Date With Mason." On a post about visiting the zoo as a family, Kim wrote,

> Yesterday the whole family took Mason to the San Diego Zoo!! . . . It's so nice to get out of LA for a short trip and spend time with Grandma MJ, who I don't get to see as much as I'd like. . . . Style Snapshot: I'm wearing J Brand leather leggings, Phillip Lim top and vintage YSL necklace.

After explicitly mentioning "family time" Kim name checks the brands she's wearing in the family photo. This post simultaneously builds the family narrative while reminding readers Kim is a celebrity, wearing expensive clothing. Moreover, the same event, like the zoo visit, is featured in multiple posts over several days, extending the authenticity of an actual occasion over a lengthy time period, exposing the fabricated nature of the authenticity building. It is difficult to ascertain exactly how much time is truly spent with family.

Moreover, various family celebrations are portrayed on the blog, further building the narrative of a supposedly very happy family. Kim marked Father's Day by disclosing her ostensibly true feelings about her family, writing, "Father's Day is always bitter sweet. Of course every year that goes by I miss my dad, but I am so blessed to have had two incredible dads. Thank you Bruce for always being there for me!" (June 17, 2012). What could be an insightful post about mourning her biological father or discussing her emotions toward Bruce is simplified into gratitude, an uncomplicated sentiment. This, along with the gallery of fifty family photos, is an easily digestible post on what could be a conflicted day. A possible moment of truth is reduced to a concept easily palatable by readers, forming an allegedly authentic, yet shallow version of herself.

Birthdays are also specifically noted. On June 27th, Kim entreated her fans to "Leave your birthday messages for Khloé in the comments!!! Xo." This post, along with the photos of her and her sister, reiterates Kim's intimate relationship with Khloé, as well as permits fans to feel as if they can communicate with Khloé as well.

Kim also constructs authenticity by portraying awkward situations or posing for amusing photos. For example, she published a photo of a ripped dress, with the description "About to do Jimmy Kimmel & my whole dress rips! Help!!! Time to sew me in . . . praying this works!" (June 17, 2012). Wardrobe malfunctions may be something to which her audience can relate, making her a more accessible and genuine person. Likewise, she posted a picture of her jokingly pretending to drink from a two-liter bottle of Orange Crush soda (August 5, 2012). Humor adds another likable facet to her personality.

Charity functions are another element of the authenticity creation. Kim occasionally posts about attending a philanthropic event or publicizes an aid organization, providing a link through which people can donate funds. In an example, on June 13 Kim published an entry titled "Dress For Success Luncheon With Mom," which featured a photo of her and her mother at a charity event. Kim captioned the photo, "Such an important cause and something that is very close to my heart as a business woman. Xo." Kim not only establishes her beneficence, but also labels herself as a "business woman," not a celebrity or reality-TV star. An entrepreneur may be an aspirational title for fans and frames Kim in a more serious light.

A final component of her authenticity construction overlaps with her celebrity construction. During the summer of 2012, Kim dated rap musician Kanye West, a globally popular acclaimed musician. Kim promulgated intimate photos of the two of them, validating the sincerity of this relationship, and displaying a tender side of herself. She posted a photo of Kanye kissing Kim in a crowd (July 13, 2012). A week later, she posted a seemingly candid photo of herself, sister Kendall, and Kanye on a rollercoaster, illustrating to readers her family's acceptance of her boyfriend (July 18, 2012). Lastly, throughout the analysis period, a series of photos were published, titled "His & Hers" that showed components of various matching outfits worn by Kim and Kanye. The first mention of Kanye on the blog is in this series. In a photo posted June 8, 2012, taken of their feet, they both wear Kanye West sneakers. In Kim's world, devotion and love are symbolized by wearing an item of clothing her boyfriend designed. Moreover, the self-taken shots apparently prove it's her blogging, revealing truthful moments from life, and reiterate her authenticity. Concurrently, Kanye's celebrity status adds to her celebrity: his presence in her photographs transfers some of his signified celebrity aura to her (Williamson, 1978).

Celebrity

A second narrative throughout her blog simultaneously provides evidence of and justifies her celebrity, akin to the Twitter lifestyle narrative. Within this narrative, Kim substantiates her fame through exhibiting images from magazine photo-shoots, visiting international locales, comparing herself to other famous beautiful women, and associating with Kanye West. While Kim bolsters her fame via drawing upon Kanye's, she also shares her fame with family members, exposing their growing celebrity to her fans, thus increasing her family's overall renown.

Images from magazine photo-shoots reiterate her fame and also privilege her fans, who are able to view the images without buying the periodicals. Almost without exception, the portraits are glamorous, showcasing Kim's face and body. Kim published multiple blog posts about her magazine cover shoots for *Esquire Latin America*, *L' Uomo Vogue*, and *InStyle UK*.

On June 25th, Kim posted a gallery of ninety-six magazine cover photos, featuring her and her sisters. Kim utilizes this celebrity to promote her business ventures and also augment family members' celebrity, via associating her fame with them and by promoting them. Not only does Kim's blog feature representations from her photoshoots, but also photographs for her various business endeavors. At various times throughout the summer she posted about new Kardashian Kollection clothing pieces and other jewelry and clothing lines. Likewise, on July 31 she wrote an entry about younger sisters Kendall and Kylie appearing on the September cover of *Seventeen*.

Kim also creates celebrity by comparing herself to other famous women, positioning herself as famous and beautiful. In separate blog posts she likened herself to Sophia Loren (July 31, 2012) and contrasted herself with Madonna (August 1, 2012). The blog post highlighting Madonna juxtaposed photos of the two celebrities at the same age. This collocation links Kim with Madonna, a global pop phenomenon, renown for her public sexual antics and indisputably incredibly famous.

Celebrity is often inextricable from wealth. Kim's celebrity is reiterated through her ability to afford high-end couture fashion, other expensive goods, and visit international locales. This may be in stark contrast to her fans' lives, who may enjoy voyeuristically viewing Kim's fabulous celebrity lifestyle. For instance, a trip to Paris Fashion Week merited numerous blog entries over June and July. One entry included a photo of her and Kanye posing in front of a white Lamborghini. Other entries featured couture clothes, such as this description "Style Snapshot: I'm wearing a Stephane Rolland dress and Christian Louboutin shoes" (July 4, 2012).

Kanye West is featured throughout the summer of 2012. As mentioned earlier, blog posts that feature Kanye West also buttress Kim's celebrity, permitting her to share in his global celebrity. His celebrity and profession add to her glamorous lifestyle, supporting her celebrity ranking. On July 6, she posted an entry containing a photo of a billboard advertising a Kanye West concert at the Revel casino in Atlantic City. Presumably her status as his girlfriend provides exclusive perks: backstage access, special treatment, and meeting other famous people. Moreover, in an overt amplification of Kim's celebrity, Kanye incorporated her into one of his music videos, which affirms and augments her fame. She promoted the video, providing a link to the video for the song "I wish you would" by DJ Khaled, Rick Ross, and Kanye West (August 14, 2012).

Behind the Scenes

A third narrative visible on the blog is that of behind-the-scenes depictions. This may supposedly reveal more of Kim's genuine life to her fans, permit them to feel connected to Kim, and joins in her Twitter feed and reality shows in illustrating Kim's "true" life.

A chief aspect of this narrative is self-titled behind-the-scenes images from photo-shoots. Several blog posts have titles akin to this, "Behind The Scenes At My Esquire Cover Shoot!" (June 1, 2012) and feature a photo of Kim typically getting her hair or makeup done or posing with a crewmember. These posts illustrate aspects of her work life and potentially may induce readers to buy the magazine for more pictures from the photo-shoot. There are several posts dedicated to behind-the-scenes illustrations of her magazine photo-shoots as well as other photography sessions. Occasionally, these entries will feature a short video in addition to stills.

In a June 11, 2012 post about her *Esquire* magazine cover shoot, she publically thanked the crew, simultaneously adding to her authentic personality, affixing characteristics of graciousness and humility to her personality, while also granting her readers behind-the-scenes knowledge. This information may help foment the fan community, linking them through exclusive insider knowledge.

Photo shoots aren't the only medium to permit behind-the-scenes glimpses. Kim also discloses behind-the-scenes footage and stills from *Keeping Up with the Kardashians*. For example, she published a picture "From Kim's Phone" of her posing with Oprah; later in the day she also issued a post entitled "Sneak Peek At Our Interview With Oprah" which actually was comprised of a promotional video and a gallery of a "bunch of screen grabs from the video" (June 14, 2012).

In fact, numerous posts reference *Keeping Up with the Kardashians*, which only dedicated fans may realize, as the entries often are not overtly labeled as such. This rewards diligent Kardashian consumers with behind-the-scenes knowledge, creating an in-the-know group. This is exemplified by Kim posting snapshots of the family's trip to the Dominican Republic, many of which reference events depicted on the two-part, vacation-focused television episode. This includes an August 10 post, which included this testimonial: "I want to give a major shout out to our amazing glam squad who came with us to The Dominican Republic!" Recognizing that the reality-TV program, purportedly depicting the real lives of the Kardashians, travels with hair and make-up staff shatters the illusion of true-to-life portrayal of perfection and sincerity, while permitting Kim's readers to be "in the know" due to Kim's behind-the-scenes revelations. Among the many posts about the vacation, Kim also recognizes the crew, expressing her appreciativeness and self-effacement, while also indicating collusion between the crew and the Kardashians.

Another interesting bit of intimate disclosure also pertained to the Dominican vacation; a behind-the-scenes perspective of a family video, which made the social media rounds. Kim posted an entry titled, "Shooting our Biggie Video" offering insider information about a popular Kardashian-created viral video (August 22, 2012). These behind-the-scenes exposés permit audience members to feel as if they are a part of Kim's celebrity life and her family, and also help sustain her fame by adding to Kim's celebrity. Moreover, while occasionally adding seemingly authentic facets to her personality, concurrently the behind-the-scenes narrative reveals the professional assistance required to attain Kim's beauty.

Beauty

Another correlated narrative is that of beauty and how to achieve it. This narrative consists of advice from professionals and Kim, as well as establishes and confirms certain standards of beauty. There are copious posts that consist solely of pictures of Kim, looking perfectly made-up and remarkably beautiful; her beauty is consistent with the American-media endorsed standard of beauty, which includes facial symmetry, heavy makeup, flawless skin, and photo-shopped imperfections. For example, such beauty-focused posts include a photo with the title "Finishing Touches" (June 1, 2012) and the next day another photo, titled "Ready for my close-up." These images help reiterate her beauty and set a standard of beauty linked to glamor and unattainable perfection.

Rob Sheppy, Kim's frequent makeup artist and hair stylist, has several guest posts on Kim's blog, each labeled "Rob Blog." Within them, Rob details how to achieve a particular look of Kim's, from clothing to hair to makeup. Rob implores readers to "Follow me on Twitter and Facebook Page: Rob Scheppy Beauty!" and then to "Click through the gallery for a step-by-step makeup break down and click here for Scott Cunha's Get the Look to read up on how he created Kim's sleek hairstyle for the premiere!" The galleries and videos provide easy steps for viewers to imitate Kim's makeup and hairstyles steps. Likewise, on July 11, Kim published a video of herself giving a lesson in facial contouring to a writer from the magazine *Harper's Bazaar Australia*, providing another useful video for her fans. These videos and galleries concomitantly add to Kim's celebrity (by assuming others would want to copy her style) and engender likability (anyone can be like her).

Kim also has a recurring feature titled "Midweek Makeup," in which she illustrates a beauty trend with several images and recommends makeup choices. Similarly, she posted a piece labeled "Trying Khroma Blue Eyeliner," which included a close-up of her eye, presumably after having used her own makeup line's eyeliner (August 25, 2012). What better way to look as beautiful as her than using her brand of makeup?

While Kim endorses standards in makeup, she also validates mainstream and couture fashion norms through her incessant cataloging of couture outfits. In almost all posts containing a photo of herself, she includes a line detailing her stylistic choices, such as this: "Style Snapshot: I'm wearing a YSL dress and Dolce Vita sandals" (June 7, 2012). These "style snapshots" typically always refer to a high-end designer, expensive and exclusive.

Another recurring posting feature is Fashion Friday, in which Kim recommends a specific fashion trend. In one of these, Kim wrote, "Nothing makes you feel more feminine and sexy than a gorgeous lace dress! Valentino has created the most stunning lace pieces this year!" (July 6, 2012). In this post, Kim advocates for a traditional view of femininity, positing in the exclamation-point-ridden post that lace, and specifically elite brand Valentino, confirms womanliness and can make any woman confident in her sexual appeal. This also obliquely espouses materialism, or the idea that buying an item makes you better than others, and overtly sanctions consumerism, in that owning this name-brand designer clothing will engender positive emotional repercussions.

Business

Another narrative present within Kim's blog concerns business. This narrative includes frequent direct-sales posts which offer photos and links, pushing audience members to watch, purchase, or otherwise consume Kardashian products, notably Kim's merchandise, goods sold in conjunction with her sisters, and the Kardashian TV series.

One recurrent blog feature is "This or That," in which Kim invites readers to choose between two of her items, asking which they prefer. In an example, she asked readers to indicate which ring they preferred by commenting on it, encouraging them to "Get voting! Xo" (June 4, 2012). The XO at the end of the message is sociable endearment, personalizing the sale pitch to seem like it's coming from a friend. Contests like these engage the audience; engagement encourages brand loyalty (Jenkins, 2006).

Kim also pushes her shoe website, ShoeDazzle. She posted about the launch of a new show line, declaring why she prefers these shows and asked readers which they liked (June 25, 2012).

Moreover, she literally sells used items from her closet, communicating with her readers about her eBay sale items. Anyone can buy an article of clothing she actually wore; Kim is literally almost selling herself. Posts about her eBay store, from which an unspecified portion of the proceeds go to charity, continued over the entire summer.

Kim also sells products in which she and her sisters share in the revenue, exhorting readers to watch the K-Dash for QVC collection sales pitch on QVC and directing them to the clothing line's online home, in order to facilitate purchasing. While convenient for her fans, this is also a blatant sales technique.

Additionally, in order to promote the Kardashian Kollection, she lists its press elsewhere. She notified readers about the Kardashian Kollection appearing on Oprah's show (August 10, 2012) and later in the month, noted that the clothing line was featured in *Cosmopolitan* and *InStyle* magazines (August 18, 2012).

Kim also posts about other celebrities wearing clothing she and her sisters designed, augmenting the line's glamorous connotations. On June 21, she pointed out pop star Carly Rae Jepson wearing clothing from the Kardashian Kollection and later in the month posted a picture of Cheryl Burke in the Kardashian Kollection as well (June 26, 2012).

Over the summer of 2012, she and her sisters relocated their L.A. area based clothing boutique, DASH. She kept readers apprised of their progress, informing readers of sales and dates of interest, such as when DASH L.A. was scheduled to open (July 11, 2012).

In another promotional mechanism that benefits her family as well as herself, Kim repeatedly peddles *Keeping Up with the Kardashians*. Any increase in ratings potentially raises advertising rates for the series, prolongs the series' longevity, and amplifies individual family members' celebrity. Under the repeated label, "KUWTK Preview," she posts brief clips of the upcoming shows, coaxing her fans to tune in.

While this business narrative primarily consists of hard sells, Kim attempts to keep her fans' interest by repeatedly linking to different websites, uploading pictures, and asserting her (always positive) opinion about the merchandise. Furthermore, the sneak peeks of the TV show may entice fans, privileging them with footage not yet aired. Finally, this narrative implicitly concludes that Kim works hard, devoting time and effort into selling her products, echoing a theme within the series.

Linked Celebrity, Business, and Family

A final narrative links three previous narratives together: celebrity, business, and family. This amalgamated classification combines aspects of all three, producing a narrative unique to the Kardashian family. Within the family unit, relationships, professional agreements, and fame creation and sustenance are synergistically bonded, symbiotically strengthening each other.

Their many family commercial ventures are exemplified in a new cosmetic enterprise, unveiled in June of 2012. A family venture amongst the sisters, Khroma Beauty connects family, commercial partnership, and fame, as indicated by the idea of being on camera or at a shoot. Without any one of these three components Khroma couldn't exist, nor the Kardashian empire.

Likewise, the Kardashian Kollection is also emblematic of this successful fusion, permitting not only domestic endeavors, but global ones as well. In August, Kim announced that the Kardashian Kollection was being offered at UK Dorothy Perkins stores, as well as in Turkey, Thailand, Malaysia, Indonesia, and Saudi Arabia (August 13, 2012). Although Kim is the most well-known Kardashian sister, she includes her sisters in her announcement. The importance of family may have international fan appeal.

This narrative also includes promotional appearances for the joint endeavors. On June 8, Kim contended that she had fun with her sisters promoting their various endeavors on the Jimmy Kimmel Live show, "I had so much fun with my sisters on Wednesday night! Did you guys watch? Jimmy was rocking his Kardashian Kolors nail polish, lol!!" By saying she has fun with her sisters, she turns a promotional appearance (even mentioning the Kardashian Kolors nail polish) into a family event, subtly changing the contextual frame from business to quality family bonding time and sisterhood. In effect Kim turns this item from a sales pitch into a family piece.

Similarly, a post about Kim's fragrance launch at the Kardashian Khaos store notes the importance of even more family, mentioning her cousin, Cici Bussey, my cousin, who runs their store in The Las Vegas Mirage casino and hotel (June 20, 2012). Kim again transforms a product placement post into an entry celebrating family, masking the true nature of her blog: to create and sustain fandom, to sell products to these fans, and to bolster Kim and her family's coffers.

Furthermore, Kim also uses this camouflaging technique to transform literal advertisements into posts focused upon family and fame. On July 10, 2012 she publicized new ads for the Kardashian Kollection, raving about how much she loved the photos. By first mentioning her sisters, then leading the next sentence with details from the photo shoot, Kim distracts readers from the content of the third sentence, which directs fans immediately to new items for sale online. She entices readers with the new photographs, encouraging them to click through and buy the products. The focus is misleading, again masterfully masking the real reason for the site's existence.

Materialism

Throughout the entire blog, two themes exist: materialism and a social-media-created community. Strewn throughout the entries are references to expensive luxury items, while Kim's sales pitches appeal to the idea of materialism, the idea that buying something makes you an inherently better person than someone who does not, elevating the consumer's socioeconomic and class status.

On June 5, 2012 Kim posted a photo of an Yves St. Laurent iPad case, featuring a high-end couture house branded gun. YSL iPad cases start at $425. A June 19 post featured pictures of Lamborghinis, while on August 16, she posted a photo of herself sitting in a Kim Kardashian branded-car, her initials monogrammed on the Bentley's headrests. The car theme continued on August 25, in a post about a new toy, referencing the 2013 G63 Mercedes, a car with a base price of $150,000.

Similarly, all of her sales pitches, disguise as family posts notwithstanding, blatantly appeal to materialism. In an example representative of many, on June 11, 2012 she extolled the virtues of her jewelry collection, saying she would wear some of it herself. She implies that by buying the pieces, the consumer will be more like Kim, raising the status of the wearer while employing the value of materialism as a selling tool.

Kim utilizes this technique as well in her eBay sales, repeatedly promoted on the blog. She promotes her personal auctions, selling items from her closet directly to fans. Fans may purchase due to her fame, selling skills, and appeal to the materialistic value of trying to better oneself through consumption.

Social Media Community

The second theme permeating the blog is that of a social-media-created fan community. Kim recognizes and encourages the online community based upon her by consistently directing attention to fans that curate online pages devoted to her and her family, singularly naming individual fans, and applauding other family members' forays into social media.

Tumblr Tuesdays are a regular highlight of Kim's blog. Tumblr is a blog-hosting platform that permits members to create and design their own blogs. On Tumblr Tuesdays, Kim asks fans who construct Kardashian-related Tumblr pages to leave their blog name in the comments. She then selects one or two of those Tumblr pages to share with her fans the following week. On June 19, 2012 she wrote: "Shout out to my Tumblr dolls!!! Found this cute pic on heckyeahkimkardashian's Tumblr [web link]! Leave your Tumblr names in the comments . . . I love looking at all your Tumblr blogs and always find so many cute pics! Xo." Directly addressing her fans, exhorting them to communicate with her, and then applauding their fandom helps build a community of Kim Kardashian fans.

The fan Tumblr pages typically are collages of numerous Kardashian photographs pulled from sundry sources. The amalgamations speak to fan interest in Kim and her family, and are a fan's method of involving him or herself in the media text through creation of ancillary media. This follows Jenkins (1992) notion of "textual poaching," in which the Kardashian fans are "insistent on making meaning from materials others have characterized as trivial and worthless" (p. 3). This meaning making in conjunction with social media-facilitated connections help build a community centered upon a common interest. Many of the fans' Tumblr names reflect their interests, including names such as MannyKardashian, Kardashian-Jenner-Klan, and iheartkimberly. Moreover, Tumblr Tuesdays generate numerous responses in the comments; the amount of Kardashian-related blogs numbers in the hundreds, if not thousands. The July 3, 2012 Tumblr Tuesdays post received over 190 comments; a normal post typically receives less than 50.

Kim also recognizes fans by noticing particular endeavors on her blog and by occasionally recognizing their contact with her on Throwback Thursdays. On Throwback Thursdays Kim posts old photos of her family. Occasionally, she finds these via Twitter fan interactions. For example, on August 23, 2012 she pointed out an old family video sent to her by @AddictedTo-KimK. Kim's selection of @AddictedToKimK's tweet and video elevates this Twitter user to a status higher than other fans; others may strive for this level of connection to Kim. Kim also singles out other fans for their dedication and Kardashian-related work. On June 11, 2012 she published a blog entry focused on two fans, Kendall and Libby Glazer, who were inspired to start their own charity after reading one of Kim's blog posts. The following month, on July 16, 2012 she directed readers to visit her fan Maytedoll's blog, dedicated to recreating Kim's fashion looks on a lower budget. Both of these Kim-created posts indicate Kim's celebrity, as without her inspiration, neither of these two endeavors would exist.

Another way Kim facilitates social-media community is by thanking her fans for their social media involvement. This demonstrates respect for them and humility on Kim's part. Near the start of the study, on June 15, 2012 Kim reached fifteen million Twitter followers and posted the following statement: "Thank you soooo much to all of my amazing Twitter followers, especially my Twitter dolls and our incredible fans around the world. I love you guys! Xo." The name endearment "dolls" signifies a label that fans can utilize to identify themselves. Moreover, thanking them and "loving" them for being fans exhibits Kim's engagement with the overall community; she realizes her fans are important. The following month Kim reached ten million Facebook "likes." Kim again thanked her fans, her dolls, and posted a gallery of all her profile pics over the years for fans to peruse. Again, the use of the pet name, doll, signifies membership in the community. By the end of this study, Kim's Twitter follower count had risen to over sixteen million.

Kim solicits fan interaction throughout the majority of blog entries. She urges fans to connect with her on Twitter, Facebook, and through the blog. In a noticeable post reflecting on her social media and its relationship with celebrity, she wrote:

> As you guys know, it's so important to me to always stay connected with my friends, family and fans online as well as offline! My family members and I put ourselves out there with our TV show, opening up our lives to the world, and our social media . . . Twitter [web link], Facebook [web link] and blogs are an extension of that! Xo (July 19)

Kim rhetorically accords her fans as much importance as her friends and family by placing them in the same sentence. Moreover, she notes that social media is another path of access to her and her family's lives, encouraging fans to join her relatives' online communities and to share her posts via social media. Social media exposure helps sustain and augment celebrity, promotes various business ventures, and may literally add to the number of fans.

DISCUSSION

This chapter explores how social media narratives contribute to the overall Kardashian celebrity and what inherent ideals influence the brand meaning. The seven blog narratives, family and authenticity, celebrity, business, behind the scenes, beauty, social media, and the amalgamated category of family/business/celebrity, are all related and reiterate celebrity status, provide authenticity, connect Kim to her fans, and support ideals of materialism. These help craft appealing markers of the Kardashian brand also found in the television series, such as sisterhood, glamour, and sincerity. Ultimately, each blog category contains many links to consume her and her family's products online, encouraging the sustenance of the Kardashian brand. Utilizing the Veblen (1899/1994) pecuniary emulation effect, Kim implicitly persuades fans that consuming her products can up their social status. In sum, Kim's blog primarily exists to promote herself, her products, and the Kardashian brand, as well as develop the fan community and amplify celebrity.

While social media fan-community members may enjoy their participation, the community primarily exists to create an audience to whom to sell more products, to be able to charge advertisers more for tweets and other social media product placement, and to increase Kardashian fame through greater recognition. Whereas the celebrity and business narratives overtly work to raise Kim's status and promote her business ventures, the behind-the-scene narrative ostensibly provides backstage knowledge to ardent fans, but truly implicitly functions as another promotional tool for the various products and media in which Kim participates.

Concurrently, Kim's blog utilizes Marwick and Boyd's (2011) means of cultivating fame via Twitter: she recognizes her fan community, publically has a relationship with them, and provides assumed intimate knowledge of herself. Within the comments associated with Kim's blog posts, fans publish their comments, alternately showing their expertise by being critical of editors and magazines, demonstrating their relationship with Kim by asking her questions and providing feedback, and connecting with each other through discussion. This online engagement helps bond users' identities to brand attributes, ensuring consumer allegiance (McClain, 2010).

On television, reality TV personalities convey authenticity through emotions and presentation of ordinariness (McClain, 2011). Kim Kardashian follows this formula through another medium: Twitter. Through her personal facts, interactions with fans, and emotional tweets she constructs an authentic persona. Particularly the tweets about her then-current boyfriend ("I miss my humpkin") were constructed to ostensibly express sincere emotions. This corresponds with various previous research (Marshall, 2010; Marwick and boyd's, 2011; Muntean and Petersen, 2009) that contends Twitter permits a seemingly authentic persona to be visible.

Kim's blog also superficially permits an "authentic celebrity voice," (Muntean & Petersen, 2009) building both sincerity and celebrity. However, Kim's blog focuses primarily upon creating, sustaining, and validating celebrity. Throughout her blog, Kim's authenticity is presented only in conjunction with her family, and not as an essential characteristic. Perhaps due to its text-based nature, Kim's Twitter account builds authenticity more effectively than the blog. Kim's blog, rife with photos of Kim stylishly attired and flawlessly made up, presents a celebrity image much more frequently than that of a down-to-earth person. Twitter, primarily consisting of words, generally absents Kim's physicality, and largely portrays her ostensibly true personality. For example, while in her blog Kim encourages consumers to buy her products, including the Kardashian Kollection clothing line, among the myriad of pictures of Kim and the plethora of sales posts she is very rarely shown actually wearing the clothing she co-designed with her sisters. She is much more likely to be wearing high-end fashion, which connotes that while anyone may buy the Kardashian Kollection to ostensibly imitate Kim and her sisters, she is too high-class and rich to wear clothing sold on QVC and in Sears. Kim simultaneously attempts to portray herself as a high-class, high-status celebrity, and as likeable and family-oriented, creating an identity fusing high and low culture. Her audience may recognize her as one of them, in that she is supportive of family and friends, yet also aspire to be famous and wealthy like her.

Within Kim's blog, Twitter feed, and *Keeping Up with the Kardashians*, the similar ideals reside: family, celebrity, and materialism. Many of the narratives throughout the blog echoed the conflated dichotomies depicted on the TV program. The authenticity narrative recalls the ideal of family, while the business narrative evokes the conflation of family and business evident in the series. The celebrity and beauty narratives resonate with similar standards within the television program. Moreover, the amalgamated narrative carries deep significance, as the synthesis of these values also appears on the program. The finding of this unification across studies and media indicates import. The Kardashians are emblematic of a shift in cultural values, retaining traditional values while incorporating new. The traditional values are represented by the prominence of family, a value that stands throughout cultures and epochs. Business and celebrity, particularly in relation to media, may be understood as values that have gained new consequence in the era of modern media, since the Industrial Revolution and rise in popularity of radio and film. This mixture of family/business/celebrity is truly what the Kardashians embody across all media.

Repetition of content across social media cements the Kardashian identity, presents a unified and coherent brand, and creates a simple salable image. Kim's Twitter feed and blog often refer to one another and are frequently linked, with tweets directing readers to the blog, and vice versa. In this sense, the Kardashian empire is an excellent example of Jenkins' (1998) notion of contemporary convergence—repetition of the same content across different media, ranging from the TV series to social media like blogs, Instagram, Twitter, and Facebook. While deeper meanings lurk underneath the shallow presentation, like the endorsement of materialism, audiences can easily understand, at least in a superficial way, who and what the Kardashians are. Downsides to this reiteration across channels include the simplification of media for the masses, the limitation of unique content, and the perpetuation of the paradigm of capitalism—which is, after all, the ultimate ideology the Kardashians epitomize.

Social media, like Twitter and her blog, helps Kim maintain and grow her fame, personal and family brand, and many revenue-producing ventures. Thus, new media helps to maintain the status quo of the importance of celebrity and individual identity. Furthermore, Twitter engenders an extremely engaged fan who aids in Kardashian's brand construction through creativity, consumption, distribution, and endorsement. By smart, interactive media use and "being herself," Kim Kardashian sustains a media empire and revamps "pointless babble" into character-constructing building blocks of celebrity, brand, and profits.

Chapter Five

Journalistic Interpretation of the Kardashians

Keeping Up with the Kardashians depicts the grasping of stardom, transparently illustrating how a kernel of fame can be developed into a far-reaching branding empire. This empire is contingent upon the legions of audience members, savvy consumers aware of media manipulation (Andrejevic, 2004). However, despite widespread knowledge of publicity maneuverings, the Kardashians have maintained a popular culture dominance, regularly appearing on magazine covers and on television. Regardless of this apparent popularity, media coverage is often adverse. This chapter explores the media backlash and paradoxical popularity.

This chapter seeks to understand how the mainstream press interprets the Kardashian cultural phenomenon. Do media recognize and call attention to the Kardashian efforts to remain in the spotlight and subsequently the hegemonic perpetuation of social and cultural mores? Or do media merely echo how the Kardashians frame their own image?

This press coverage narrative analysis performs various functions: it contextualizes the Kardashians within a particular time frame, reveals public opinion, and explores media interpretation of the Kardashian-proffered image.

This investigation finds that 2011 news discourse encompasses diverse narratives regarding the Kardashians. These narratives concern body image, family relationships, social media, branding and business, popularity, and the marriage and divorce of Kim Kardashian and Kris Humphries. An overt tone of negativity directed toward the family is prevalent. Additionally, a consequence of the Kardashian media dominance is the repurposing of the word Kardashian; the term Kardashian is used as a synecdoche for all reality TV stars, whose fame derives from a combination of uninhibited exposure and normality. Other uses include neologistic alternate meanings.

THEORETICAL FRAMEWORK

News not only relates information, but also interprets, apprising audiences how to understand reality (Bird and Dardenne, 1988). Media often select a dominant framing, or understanding of a story, proffering a single interpretation over others. This dominant framework of understanding affects how people comprehend culture.

Within news, repetition and familiarity of narratives construct a believable reality (Barthes, 1977; Zelizer, 1997). People are exposed to news tropes and narratives throughout their lives, in myriad media forms. These narratives combine to form ideologies, or paradigms of understanding. Audiences understand daily lives, relationships, and activities through a reality that is, in part, established by media discourses. Stories and narratives within media "are symbolic actions that create social reality" (Sillars and Gronbeck, 2001, p. 215). Through these narratives, audiences learn about culture (Sillars and Gronbeck, 2001). Dominant narratives naturalize ideology and teach a moral version of reality (White, 1987). The dominant narratives, or preferred meanings, resonate in people's lives, corresponding with ideals and meanings already in place.

The 2011 news coverage is scrutinized for its significance in the Kardashian media life. Kim Kardashian was engaged, married, and separated in 2011. Additionally, in 2011 three Kardashian TV series aired, Kourtney Kardashian announced her second pregnancy, Rob Kardashian participated in *Dancing With The Stars*, and the Kardashian family was featured in Barbara Walter's annual *Most Fascinating People* television special.

In 2011, the fifth season of *Keeping Up with the Kardashians* received much media attention, as did the second season of *Kourtney and Kim Take New York* and *Khloé and Lamar*. Interestingly, due to Khloé Kardashian's husband Lamar's occupation as a professional basketball player, the program received notice in sports columns, much of it questioning if the show would detrimentally impact his playing and how much revenue he earned from it (e.g., Ding, 2011). Other news coverage included reviews, commentary, and human-interest pieces.

A search of the word Kardashian within the Newspapers Plus database (searching over 150 newspapers, television programs, etc.) returned 5,197 items. I perused at least one out of every ten pieces, searching for patterns, themes, and recurrences. For comparison sake, a search of the word Kardashian within the Newspapers Plus database for the year 2007, the initial year *Keeping Up with the Kardashians* aired, returned ninety-three items. The surfeit of 2011 materials in which Kardashian appears indicates their massive popularity. Articles included in this study appeared in conventional newspapers like *The New York Times, The Washington Post, USA Today,* and *The Toronto Star,* while television coverage included programs such as *Good Morning America* and CNN's *Showbiz Tonight.* Celebrity-focused magazines, such as *US Weekly* and *InTouch* magazines, were not considered. This study analyzed mainstream press coverage, which included trend pieces (typically featuring interviews), reviews, and commentary. Various types of press exist for different purposes. For example, talk-show interviews primarily provide publicity, while commentary and reviews offer critiques. The myriad forms of journalism coalesce into an overall news discourse.

The popular press analysis uncovered six narratives: body image, popularity, family relationships, social media, branding and business, and the marriage and impending divorce of Kim Kardashian and Kris Humphries. Moreover, throughout coverage an overt attitude of condemnation is rampant. Finally, linguistic implications of the varied usages of the Kardashian name are explored.

Popularity

A prominent narrative throughout the press coverage is the intense Kardashian popularity, and disdain toward it. Reporters speculate about why the Kardashians remain popular, particularly in light of their "lack of talent." Variations on the phrase "famous for doing nothing" are ubiquitous throughout the bewildered and unsympathetic news discourse, and yet concurrently "the Kardashian family is a reality TV sensation" (de Bertodano, 2011).

Documentation of Kim's popularity in particular appeared across a range of media. Many articles noted that in 2010, Kim Kardashian was the "top personality" searched on Google (Lee, Newton, and Temple, 2011) and the most searched for term on the Bing search engine (de Bertodano, 2011). She was twice the topic of questions on the NPR program *Wait, Wait, Don't Tell Me!* Lesser known celebrities long to be in "the same league as international cover girl Kim Kardashian" (Reines, 2011). Host A.J. Hammer asserted on CNN's *Showbiz Tonight,* "I think people are genuinely fascinated with Kim Kardashian" (Hammer, Wynter, and Moos, 2011). Similarly, *The Philadelphia Inquirer* television critic David Hiltbrand (2011) averred, "It's impossible to keep up with Kim Kardashian. She's rocketed into some dimension of fame far beyond reality star. You cannot go two minutes anymore without seeing her name or image."

Taking note of the many fans also emphasized popularity. For example, a long line of autograph seekers greeted Kim in Las Vegas (Perez-Feria, 2011) and the family won the Choice TV Female Reality/Variety Star at the Teen Choice Awards (Teen Choice Award Winners, 2011).

Along with popularity substantiation, media critiqued the Kardashian fame. Rich Juzwiak avowed in *The Washington Post*, "Their legion of admirers notwithstanding, there is something about the Kardashians' brand of celebrity that disgruntles those who aren't riding their train."

Others scornfully noted the Kardashians are well-known for their seemingly ordinary lives. The irony of this normality is not unnoticed:

> Their lives—complete with their fabulous mansions, their Bentleys, their pool houses—are so far removed from those of their viewers and so out of sync with the rest of the recession-hit world that it is like watching an episode of Dallas or Dynasty. The icing on the cake is that this family is "real." (de Bertodano, 2011)

Despite this fame, writer Rebekah Devlin wondered, "I mean, why do we want to see former Spice Girl Mel B brushing her children's hair, or the Kardashians going shopping? . . . Boring parts of life are boring . . . no matter who does them" (2011). As Kim herself said to Barbara Walters, "I think it's more of a challenge for you to go on a reality show and get people to fall in love with you for being you. So there's definitely a lot more pressure, I think, to be famous for being ourselves than to play a character" (Walters, 2011).

Another writer opined about Kim's popularity during her foray into the music industry, "Sadly, Kim's song will be successful even if it is atrocious . . . we're happy to encourage people with no talent in a field they are obscenely underqualified for" (Foster, 2011). While the Kardashian celebrity may be unwarranted by obvious talent, they remain popular nevertheless, a fact media despairingly reported.

Body Image

Throughout the press coverage there is a consistent focus on the Kardashian sisters' body image, with specific emphasis on Kim Kardashian's build. Kim is hailed as representative of a fuller figure than has been popular in the recent past. According to *The Sydney Sunday Telegraph* "There's little doubt that the sexy reality television star brought curves back into style this year with her pneumatic figure" (Domjen and Moran, 2011). One newspaper article noted Kim posed nude or practically naked several times: a 2007 *Playboy* spread, a cover photo for *W Magazine* in November 2011, and a photoshoot in April 2011's *Harper's Bazaar* (Kim Says She's No Sex Symbol, 2011). Moreover, "The fact that Kim has a very un-Hollywood silhouette is one of the reasons people find it easy to relate to her" regardless of her fame (de Bertodano, 2011).

Kim's sex symbol status due to her body and frequent nudity is duly noted. On *CNN*, Kim noted, "It's a part of my personality, for sure, and I definitely play it up a lot" (Hammer, Winter, and Moos, 2011). Kim explained in another source that being a sex symbol is "definitely powerful" (Derakhshani, 2011). Indeed, a rash of stories appeared frequently referencing Kim's "bodacious backside" upon the death of a young woman while receiving an illegal buttock-enhancing medical procedure (Burling, 2011). Articles concerning this death typically noted Kim's position as a sex symbol and body image role model.

Despite being known for her sex appeal, Kim repeatedly complained in the press of being "insecure." She asserted, "I don't find myself as sexy as everyone thinks" and "I'm a lot more insecure than people would assume" (Kim Says She's No Sex Symbol, 2011). Perhaps Kim is insecure because of jokes like this one, which occurred in a Canadian newspaper: "The Kardashian sisters are planning to launch their own clothing line at Sears later this year. The clothes will come in three sizes: Kourtney, Kim and Khloé" (The Monday File, 2011).

Khloé Kardashian, the tallest and biggest sister, is often hounded for her weight online and in tabloid magazines. In an interview with Barbra Walters, Khloé asserted, "the internet could be so negative. They call me Shrek or an ogre, they're awful to me" (2011). The press, however, joins the voice of her mother, Kris Jenner, who suggested Khloé lose weight on *Keeping Up with the Kardashians*, to which Khloé reacted with anger. On *Good Morning America*, Khloé addressed this, defending her mother, "she's my mom, but she's also my manager at the same time" and thus must try to promote what she thinks is best for Khloé's career (2011, June 6). In another piece, Khloé noted, "Dealing with the Kardashian body image is hard. Kim and Kourtney have said to me, 'If we were put under the same negative attention you are, we couldn't handle it'" (Bardon, 2011).

The body image narrative overtly echoes a Kardashian television show thesis, that the Kardashian body is attainable through plastic surgery and products. As one article noted, "Kardashian-backed products all promise swift defeat for a burgeoning mid-section" (Gordon, 2011). Furthermore, when body image is considered in conjunction with the branding narrative discussed later, it seems that the sexual Kardashian body ideal is achievable to consumers simply through purchasing Kardashian-endorsed clothing, fragrances, and other products. The insecurity Kim exhibits also appears in the series, underscoring Kim's seeming normality through shared emotions. This humility may endear her to audiences.

Family Relationships

Another narrative prevalent throughout the news discourse is the too tightly-knit nature of the Kardashian family, even as they disagree and quarrel. On *Good Morning America*, Khloé Kardashian asserted, "we genuinely love each other, and like, my sisters are my best friends." The sisters agreed with host Robin Roberts's description of their familial relationships: "nothing really is off bounds when it comes to you and the family" (2011).

Oldest sister Kourtney Kardashian exemplifies the closeness of the family in this printed statement about her son, Mason, "Unless I'm working, I can't be away from him without feeling guilty. It doesn't feel good or natural to be, so it's a struggle." She continued,

> I don't want to judge, but I've also met women who think it's cool to be out or away from their baby, and I don't get that. Every time I'm not working, he's with me. Even on an airplane, he is with me even if the nanny is also on the plane. Any time I can have with him, I am lucky to have. (Separation Anxiety Haunts Kourtney, 2011)

Elsewhere in the press, Khloé epitomized the self-proclaimed lovingness among the family, saying she is most proud of "my family, just how close we are and supportive of one another." Mom Kris agreed, saying, "I'm just proudest of my kids. I feel like the most blessed mom alive, because I get to get up every day and work with my family. And it doesn't get any better than that" (Walters, 2011). Similarly, when asked what her deceased father would think of the family today, Kim replied: "He would be so proud of all of us. Individually and how we work together, because we represent what he always taught us—that family is everything" (de Bertodano, 2011).

During the autumn of 2011, Rob Kardashian participated on the reality competition program *Dancing With The Stars*. The family supported him, as Khloé stated on *Good Morning America*, "I'm like, I'm gonna be your stage mom and I'm gonna make sure that you're actually like, he needs to like just get it together and have confidence. I said no one's expecting you to be a professional dancer, but try your hardest" (2011, September 7).

However, media labeled the Kardashian family's intimate nature as too close. For example, *The Hamilton Spectator* noticed that Kourtney and her partner, Scott, "have even stopped enjoying having date nights together because they miss Mason so much" (Separation Anxiety Haunts Kourtney, 2011). The familial nature of the group may inhibit individual relationships.

Arguments are also a consequence of having their lives overly integrated. While arguments occur on the reality shows, Khloé asserted on *Good Morning America* that the press prefers to highlight the arguments rather than the familial bonds. According to Khloé, if all three sisters were to be pregnant at the same time, the magazines would portray this "like we're competitive, and we're this and that. It's like, it's so positive and I hate how they make such a good thing into something negative" (2011, September 7).

However, the Kardashians do not lack control over all aspects of their media coverage. In an illustration of the family's savvy media manipulation, one month after the revelation of Kim's imminent divorce, Kourtney announced her second pregnancy. This changed the prevailing Kardashian news narrative from that of a failed marriage to a joyful family addition. Kourtney was quoted in an Associated Press article, which appeared throughout many sources, as saying, "You're supposed to wait twelve weeks to tell people, but I feel confident" (Kourtney Kardashian expecting baby No. 2, 2011). Apparently the need to modify the media's perception could no longer wait.

The Kardashians' familial relationships noted in the press mimic non-famous people's off-screen domestic relationships. Family members sometimes bicker. This narrative emphasizes the normality of the Kardashian clan, providing more reasons for audience approval. This narrative also provides an aspirational familial model for audiences; they may admire and covet the Kardashian family's intimacy and affection. Ironically, the Kardashians rely on the press coverage to escalate fame while lamenting the negativity within it.

Social Media

Media also highlights the family's, and particularly Kim's, social media use as popularity evidence and means of augmentation. In 2011, Kim ranked as the sixth most followed Twitter user in the world (Leonhardt, 2011). Press commentary within this narrative focuses on two components of social media use: Kim's Twitter popularity and how social media affects the Kardashian brand.

For example, CNN host Piers Morgan (2011) humorously implored Kim and Khloé to ask their followers to follow him. Each has a significant amount of followers, with Kim's totaling more than thirteen million at the time. Moreover, a substantial amount of articles discussed the business of being paid to tweet to those followers, for instance, describing how the company Ad.ly matches celebrities to products and often writes product placement tweets in the voice of celebrity clients (Coyle, 2011). Kim is Ad.ly's most-followed client and her tweets are regularly retweeted (posted again) by at least fifty other people (Burns, 2011). Kim's social media influence is associated with her Twitter-facilitated fan interaction (Leonhardt, 2011). In a compelling example of her influence, the Los Angeles Police Department asked Kim to tweet about the 405 Freeway closure (Lang, 2011).

The press coverage noted in amazement the amount of sundry brands exploiting Kim's social media popularity across varied platforms. In an example of a social media advertising campaign, Kim's Sketchers sneakers endorsement included television commercials, Facebook ads, and an online contest to win a workout session with her (Horovitz, 2011). Kim also tweeted about the sneakers. Other Kardashians employ social media for profit as well; a tweet produced by Khloé can cost a company around $8,000 (Rexrode, 2011).

According to many articles, the Kardashian brand also benefits from their social media shrewdness. The sisters crowd-sourced a title for their novel, asking fans to submit potential titles online (Novel Idea: Fans Get To Name Kardashian Book, 2011). Many reports remarked upon Kim's promotion of wedding-associated products through her Twitter feed and blog, such as "her pre-wedding workouts (with celebrity trainer Gunnar Peterson), her dress fittings (with designer Vera Wang), and her invitation designer (Lehr & Black)" (Cohen, 2011). Fans could also sign a virtual guestbook on her website (Cohen, 2011).

The press coverage explains how the Kardashians' social media engagement not only creates revenue for the Kardashians, but augments their popularity as well. Social media is another venue to create and feed fans' appetites for Kardashian material. Generally, the press coverage's tone of this social media savvy is one of astonishment. The fourth estate marvels at just how perceptively the Kardashians understand their audience. Kim Kardashian is often presented as an exemplary model of social media brand building and celebrity amplification.

Business and Branding

A facet of celebrity is a successful brand and correlated income. Fittingly, the most dominant narrative within the news discourse concerns the Kardashian business acumen, particularly focusing upon the immense success of the Kardashian brand, albeit from a pejorative perspective. Notably, a profusion of articles reported in wonderment that the Kardashian family earned a reported $60 million dollar income in 2010. As CNN Host Piers Morgan (2011) said, "they've managed to build a multimillion-dollar fortune despite having no discernible ability other than a brilliant talent for self-promotion. There's no denying their power as celebrity brands."

The Kardashians earn money through simply "being themselves," something the press struggles to clarify. As Richard Perez-Feria (2011) elucidated:

> Kim Kardashian—and her endless stream of camera-ready relatives—made a not insubstantial $60 million in 2010. Kim Kardashian doesn't sing, doesn't act, doesn't have traditional artistic aspirations and still made more money than anyone you know—by a lot. Perfumes, beauty lines, clothing stores, commercial endorsements and, most importantly, the litany of Kardashian branded reality television programs on E! have all contributed to the truly enviable Kardashian empire.

One key element of the Kardashian empire is their vast array of product endorsements, including orange juice, jewelry, shoes, candles, perfumes, Silly Bandz, Sugar Factory candy stores, Nivea skin creams, self-tanning lotion, and diet products, among others. In an article focused upon Kim, de Bertodano (2011) claimed, "What she has successfully engineered is a commodification of the public obsession with her, forging a connection between her image and whatever product she is trying to sell" (de Bertodano, 2011).

This connection helps sell Kardashian-produced merchandise as well. In 2011, journalists detailed many of the family's new business ventures: a Sears clothing line, a Las Vegas lifestyle store dubbed Kardashian Khaos, and an ill-fated prepaid debit card. The Kardashian Kard was widely disparaged throughout news coverage for its predatory user terms. Connecticut Attorney General Richard Blumenthal averred the card was "particularly troubling because of its high fees combined with its appeal to financially unsophisticated young adult Kardashian fans" (Singletary, 2011). The Kardashians ultimately withdrew from the endorsement deal, prompting a $75 million lawsuit, which was later dismissed. This venture was a rare misstep in their business perspicacity and brand associations.

In a lengthy interview with a British newspaper, Kim discussed her brand and her audience: "I think of myself as a brand for them" (de Bertodano, 2011). Kim justified her intense self-promotion by claiming it as an expertise, saying, "if I had a great voice or was a great actress, that would be amazing. But I'm realistic: my skill and my talent is marketing." She continued, noting, "You don't just show up—there's a lot of work in building a brand. I'm involved in every last step, whether it's designing ad campaigns or saying we should launch my product here, not there" (de Bertodano, 2011).

However, others claimed the brand wouldn't exist without the flagship *Keeping Up with the Kardashians* program: "Their show is a self-perpetuating machine: It made these family members famous and got them deals and endorsements, which then provide story lines for the show, making them more famous, getting them more deals and endorsements, etc" (Juzwiak, 2011). Thus, their fame is cyclical, and to paraphrase Boorstin (1961/1992), they're famous for being famous.

In a compelling example of a direct relationship between popularity and money, Kim Kardashian earns about $75,000 for each personal domestic nightclub appearance (Goldberg, 2011). As Goldberg (2011) observed, "Celebrities attract crowds, plain and simple. They also draw paparazzi and can result in lucrative publicity for a club if photos from an event wind up in gossip magazines."

Furthermore, a considerable number of articles detailed the financial arrangements of Kim and Kris Humphries's lavish wedding, short-lived marriage, and unceremonious separation. Once news of the divorce broke, many media outlets questioned the effect of it upon the Kardashian brand. Would audiences construe "the wedding as a for-profit publicity stunt" (Stelter,

2011) and react poorly? This perception was mitigated by a statement released by E!, which in part read: "Any insinuation that E! and producers orchestrated Kim's wedding is completely false" (de Moraes, 2011).

With this firm denial spread throughout media, many journalists predicted no dire brand consequences for the assumed backlash. Reputation.com spokesman and public relations expert Howard Bragman was quoted in *USA Today*, saying, "Kim has this knack for turning the bad moments in her life into financial bonanzas." In the same article Rebecca Bienstock, deputy news director of *Us Weekly* magazine, asserted "Divorce won't hurt her popularity, and it might even be helpful . . . Everyone is going to want to see who she'll date next, and it will be the same cycle again: Dating, marriage, baby" (Puente, 2011).

Indeed, "because the family's brand feeds on drama, it's likely to absorb the shock." Moreover, the resultant publicity could help drive web traffic higher, potentially aiding sales of the Sears Kardashian clothing line (Villarreal and Tschorn, 2011).

The tone of the business-related coverage was markedly critical. For example, The Associated Press published this assessment: "The Kardashians are a great example of, in my mind, talentless celebrities, or celebrity for celebrity's sake, who took advantage of their looks, a sex tape, a lot of pretty raw and low-level stuff that titillated and fascinated the American public," said Eli Portnoy, a marketing and branding expert (Few Can Keep Up With . . .).

The news discourse acknowledged the great achievement the Kardashians have attained: a multi-million dollar branding empire built upon reality television. However, as a whole, the news industry disdained the foundation of this empire, deploring its tawdry beginnings, pandering to teens, and seeming lack of institutional deference. This disrespectful, while awed, perspective of the Kardashian accomplishments is evident in the critical approach within the great majority of coverage.

Kris and Kim: The Wedding

A prevailing narrative throughout the 2011 press coverage of the Kardashian family concerned Kim and Kris Humphries's engagement, nuptials, and divorce, with a particular focus upon the financial windfall associated with the wedding.

In May 2011, Kris Humphries popped the question with a 16.5 carat emerald-cut diamond ring, reportedly worth $2 million (Hammer, 2011a). On *Showbiz Tonight*, discussing the ring, Rachel Zalis, a contributing editor at *Life and Style Weekly* magazine, noted "And the Kardashians are marketing machines. The bigger the ring, the bigger the wedding, the bigger the story, the more money." The wedding was never evaluated in terms of love and romance; rather, almost every single news story is focused on the marriage's financial implications.

In an article titled, "Kim Kardashian's Weekend Nuptials Aren't Just a Wedding, They're an Enterprise," writer Sandy Cohen (2011) noted the "made-for-TV celebration of love, devotion and product-placement" had its expenses "offset by the bouquet of wedding deals now in place." Indeed, Kim lauded many wedding vendors in her Twitter feed and blog, triggering reporters to wonder how much the wedding really cost the Kardashians. Media reported Kim and Kris received at least the "three Vera Wang dresses Kardashian wore during the ceremony and reception, worth $20,000 each, $400,000 in Perrier Jouet Champagne, and $10,000 worth of wedding invitations." Moreover, *People* supposedly paid "$2.5 million for the exclusive rights to wedding photos and a further $300,000 for the engagement shots," while "*OK!* magazine is said to have paid $100,000 for exclusive pictures of the bridal shower." Kim also directly profited from the release of a bridal-themed limited edition perfume, named "Love." Finally, the couple also reportedly earned $15 million from E! for broadcasting their vows (Profitable Union).

Numerous media outlets reported over 500 people attended the wedding, including celebrities such as Justin Bieber, Christina Aguilera, Serena and Venus Williams, Kelly Osbourne, Demi Lovato, Mario Lopez, Eva Longoria, Sugar Ray Leonard, Alan Thicke, Lindsay Lohan, and Ryan Seacrest, as well as the roster of the New Jersey Nets (Spencer, 2011). The two-part wedding event special, *Kim Kardashian's Fairytale Wedding,* garnered 10.5 viewers for the E! network (Goldberg, S. 2011).

While the Kardashians christened Kim's nuptials "fairytale," the press continually labeled it "royal," comparing it to Prince William and Kate Middleton's wedding, which had occurred in April of the same year. Many elements of the wedding were labeled royal: the cake, the dress, and Kim's tastes. Media outlets from *USA Today* to NPR referenced the "American royal wedding"—some more tongue-in-cheek than others. *USA Today* noted, "Another royal wedding took place Saturday night"—reality-TV royalty, that is" (Clark, 2011).

This interaction occurred on CNN's *Showbiz Tonight*:

> Host A.J. Hammer: "So Carrie, to you, is it such a stretch to think that perhaps the Kardashians are indeed the royals of this country?"
> Carrie Keagan, host of VH1's *Big Morning Buzz Live*: "God. Really? Do we have to say that? But I guess it might be true. And nothing says romance like a two-part special on E."

As a British newspaper noted, "There will undoubtedly be one similarity to the royal wedding: it will be beamed into living rooms all over the world" (de Bertodano, 2011).

Despite the auspicious beginning of a televised ceremony, many journalists professed not to be surprised when the marriage ended, and claimed to have doubted its veracity from the romance's start. As ABC news reporter John Donvan (2011) explicated on *Nightline*:

> Consider, a sex tape made her famous. Big scandal, big fame, followed by big money, with the modeling jobs and the acting gigs, a perfume line. . . . Magazine covers and all of it predicated, all of it predicated on enough of us giving a hoot about this. No hoot, no loot. Here's the thing, though. Happily ever after, boring. Divorce, opens the door to whole new chapters. So, was it in the script all along?

Howard Bragman, Reputation.com spokesman and public relations expert, responded, "I think everybody saw this coming. I think Stevie Wonder saw this coming. There's lots of cynicism and doubt about the marriage to begin with. Yes, this is no big surprise."

The great majority of news outlets covering the wedding treated it sardonically, as if bewildered as to why it was necessary to report on the event. Most news outlets seemed fascinated by the costly wedding details, disregarding the values inherent within a marriage. Love was typically mentioned as only the name of Kim's newest perfume. The divorce, on the other hand, was gleefully reported, typically with a derisive smile and tenor.

Negativity

As may be plain from the evidence discussed earlier, the overwhelming tone of the news discourse was derogatory. For instance, as Barbara Walters stated upon announcing the Kardashian family as a choice for her most fascinating people special, "I have never heard more anger and dismay than when we announced that the people you're about to see were on our list. I mean, last year, we had the cast of *Jersey Shore* and no one said a word" (2011).

Several journalists decried the vapidity of the programs. In *The Sydney Morning Herald*, a reporter averred, "Only the slow-witted can keep up with the Kardashians and co." (Ritchie, 2011). Another writer described the program as depicting "high-pitched, big-butted bimbos go[ing] about their insanely unrealistic lives" (Tucker-Evans, 2011).

Sports reporters wondered why Lamar Odom would join the reality-TV genre: "I'll never understand why anyone would invest any time in the nauseating Kardashian family" (Jenkins, B., 2011). Others noted Lamar's wife, Khloé, is not welcome at certain basketball games (Inside Track, 2011).

To some, the Kardashians represent the general degeneration of American society. *The New York Times* claimed "pop culture has slid so far into the slough of celebrity worship and escapist fluff that the antics of the Kardashian sisters now pass as entertainment" (Kakutani, 2011). Others believe the Kardashians helped cause the deterioration. According to Juzwiak (2011), the Kardashians lower American behavioral standards through their "too-much-information aesthetic" or oversharing of the better-left-unseen minutiae of life. They may seem benign, however, they contribute to "loosening cultural mores," such as laxity in attitude toward plastic surgery, public nudity, and general depravity.

As mentioned previously, the wedding was often discussed in a tone of disgust. Jessica Coen, editor of the website Jezebel.com, stated on NPR's *Tell Me More*:

> [The wedding] is so over-the-top and extravagant that it's this perfect storm of our tabloid culture and the materialistic culture and then what you see every afternoon on TLC, which is this obsession with dream weddings. And here it is all coming together in this incredibly . . . borderline disgusting way. (Martin, 2011)

Upon news of the divorce, Lisa de Moraes of *The Washington Post* suggested *"Kim's Nightmare Divorce: A Kardashian Event* is a much sexier name for the next four-hour TV special than *Kim's Nightmare Annulment"* (2011).

Despite the press's apparent dislike of the family, the Kardashians remain ubiquitous throughout contemporary American society. Perhaps people don't like to admit they enjoy watching the programs, reading about the sisters in magazines, and consuming Kardashian-related news. This would explain the People's Choice Award *Keeping Up with the Kardashians* won: Favorite TV Guilty Pleasure.

Linguistics

The Kardashian press coverage analysis revealed the family's popularity has spawned new, commonly understood meanings and usages of the name. As Richard Perez-Feria contended in *The Las Vegas Sun*, "The very term 'Kardashian' became a punch line (and an unflattering adjective) minimizing some well-known person's talent or shelf life in the spotlight."

Kardashian is also often used a synecdoche for all reality TV celebrities. *The Washington Post* published an article denouncing the state of American entertainment, titled "A world without the Kardashians." While this article does literally refer to the Kardashian family, the writer is also using the term to stand in for the surplus of reality television celebrities, without whom, the author contends, America would be better.

The name is also used to connote a certain kind of intense popularity. In an example, while discussing Queen Elizabeth II of England, a marketing expert was quoted as saying, "She may not be a Kardashian, but the Queen certainly has an Australian following" (Popularity reigns supreme, 2011).

Kim Kardashian is also used as a celebrity benchmark throughout unrelated press. For instance, in an article about apples, Primis (2011) stated: "The Honeycrisp has become the Kim Kardashian of the apple world: It came out of nowhere, relatively recently (it was released commercially in the 1990s), and with some marketing brilliance, took the fruit world by storm."

The appellation also functions as an adjective. For example, in the Style section of *The New York Times*, actress Debi Mazar described her fashion as "cool vintage or modern pieces that are affordable without looking too 'Kardashian'" (Chang, 2011). It is assumed readers will understand the reference.

DISCUSSION

The 2011 Kardashian press coverage analysis revealed six narratives amalgamated across media formats: body image, popularity, family relationships, social media, branding and business, and the marriage and divorce of Kim Kardashian and Kris Humphries. Throughout these six areas of coverage, the prevailing attitude was one of disapproval and censure. Finally, this analysis also disclosed neologisms of the Kardashian name.

Many of the news coverage narratives, particularly those concerning family relationships, branding and business, and body image reflect ideals and events present in the shows and in the family's social media use. Concepts the family illustrates within the program are reiterated within the press, cyclically perpetuating Kardashian-initiated characteristics. For instance, as the family presents the idea that they are a tightly knit and loving group, media repeats and validates this idea. Repetition of concepts and narratives throughout media establish ideology and educate consumers about societal norms (White, 1987). While stressing the importance of a heterosexual, white family norm may seem innocuous, it does carry some potential repercussions. Similarly, critics may deplore the unmarried status of Kourtney and the seeming abuse of the sanctity of marriage demonstrated by Kim. Regardless, press coverage helps set cultural standards, as well as reflecting the altering mores of the time period. Not one article mentioned the interracial component of Khloé and Lamar's marriage; what once would have been decried in the press doesn't merit a mention today.

Additionally, throughout the series, the theme of materialism and consumerism is vaunted. The press coverage implicitly critiques the Kardashian urge to consume through its negative tenor, particularly as related to Kim's wedding. This wedding narrative laments Kim's ability to use endorsements to apparently receive wedding materials gratis. The extravagant wedding is depicted as flashy and a bid for attention. However, by continually providing the Kardashian family and their events publicity, media obliquely perpetuates the ideals the family represents and inculcates.

Thus, journalists accept the fodder presented within the shows and press releases for use, while concurrently adding a deleterious component to the Kardashian image. Throughout the news discourse, reporters seemingly struggle to understand why audiences venerate the Kardashians, buy their products, and watch their shows, contributing to the Kardashian celebrity and brand. The press doubts the Kardashians' authenticity, notably the motives driving Kim's marriage, while also marveling at their social media brand building. They recognize the celebrity exists, yet continue to disapprove of Kardashian fame. A Kardashian media backlash exists, yet seemingly has not harmed the brand, judging by the series' high ratings, the continuation of new product endorsements, and the family members participation in new avenues of media.

Inherent sexism and classism may also play a role in the condemnation of the Kardashian empire. The Kardashians are comprised of a strong, independent matriarchy. There is also still a level of intrinsic classism within American culture, particularly evident in "high-culture" news coverage. Despite the reality television genre's success and apparent permanence within programming schedules, reality television still rouses antipathy in critics. Journalists also deplored the Kardashians' exploitation of sexuality as a transit to fame.

To answer the questions posed earlier in this chapter, media do call attention to Kardashian efforts to remain in the public eye. However, despite the vitriol directed at the Kardashians, hardly any journalists take this opportunity to emphasize the hegemonic perpetuation of cultural mores visible within the Kardashian embrace of sexuality, celebrity, and materialism. Instead, a contradiction exists between the culturally vaunted trait of American ambition (exemplified by the Kardashians) and the schadenfreude characteristic of the negative coverage. The press uniformly disparages potentially positive Kardashian qualities, like entrepreneurship, industriousness, and family. Thus, even while demonizing ostensible publicity stunts, media merely echo certain aspects of how the Kardashians present themselves: famous, fashionable, and self-obsessed.

Of course, while media discourse may help shape and reflect a public image, the Kardashians realize this is changing. As Kim noted to reporter de Bertodano (2011), "Whatever was printed [in the newspapers] used to be the last word," says Kim. "But it's not like that anymore. I can get on Twitter and have a say, too, if I feel like it."

Chapter Six

Conclusion

By recognizing and examining the pervasiveness of the Kardashians through-out American culture, this book examines the norms and codes the Kardash-ian media and brand truly present. Moreover, as a media studies scholar, I focus on the societal role the Kardashian media inhabit in order to investigate American culture. Thus, this book studies various components of the Kar-dashian empire in order to discern what this transmedia popular culture spec-tacle connotes about American society. Through analysis of heterogeneous media, including the namesake TV series, social media, and press coverage, this book details characteristic findings of the Kardashian media and image complexities. Ideals and standards the family embodies indicate societal benchmarks, what greater culture accepts and rejects, and signifies potential adaptations of the status quo. Like all families, various members' personal-ities shift and relationships fluctuate over time; however, television tends to simplify off-screen complexities into easily understood black and white val-ues. The absence of shades of gray starkly reveals stereotypes and provides fodder for conflict, allowing for easy resolutions. The outcomes permit dual ideas to exist simultaneously, providing illogicalities audiences must navi-gate, emblematic of such ironies present in everyday life.

These intrinsic paradoxes illustrated within the program include sexuality and conservatism, family and business, beauty and unhappiness, narcissism and celebrity, intimate and transgressive family nature, and traditional and nontraditional gender roles. Additionally, materialism, public vs. private sphere, and body image themes are present throughout the profusion of Kar-dashian media. The finding of these ideas across sundry media (television, print, and online) establishes their significance. The Kardashians' world, while most likely extremely different from most middle and lower class families, is replete with the representational challenges many people face in attempting to balance their own lives. From the Kardashians' representation, much can be discerned about American life and its value system.

The Kardashians give meaning to their brand through the television series and social media; the ideals connoted on television and online add significance to their image. The high ratings and their prominence throughout today's media landscape indicate the American public's acceptance of this brand, with its characteristics of wealth, glamor, sexuality, celebrity, and family. Indeed, the Kardashian brand rests upon solidarity; unity is necessary to create a cohesive brand. Each family member exhibits similar qualities and follows the family directive: all must participate in various media, provocatively exposing themselves.

While the television series may have been enough to instigate the Kardashian brand, the construction, development, and maintenance of brand and celebrity has been immensely aided by astute social media use. The numerous social media avenues provide opportunities to create layers of fun tidbits, provocative photos, and authentic sound bites, fodder for a hungry audience, keeping the brand in prime position within audience minds. Through the multitude of social media the Kardashian brand is always available for consumption.

This book encompasses an assessment of conceptual value contradictions, an exploration of varied themes, and an evaluation of the Kardashian social media-fueled celebrity. This triangulated, multimedia approach facilitates an in-depth analysis of assorted media and portrayed standards and inconsistencies, as well as the principles inherent within the family itself. Academically, by providing a fresh amalgamation of theory and analysis, this book adds to the fields of media studies, celebrity, American studies, television, and new media.

Furthermore, this book not only examines media content, but also explores how the Kardashians exploit media for profit in today's neoliberal American and global economy. The study of the family's exceptional multimodal utilization of traditional media (television, print) and social media (Twitter, blogging) demonstrates how capitalism and its corollary values manifest throughout the Kardashian-produced media. Their online public sphere operations are governed by the off-line economic value system visible in their television programs. Via interactive media and "being their selves," the Kardashians renovate banal status updates and hackneyed reality television into character-constructing building blocks of brand, celebrity, and profits. This media exploitation is an exemplar of the intricate new media capitalization model.

FINDINGS

Chapter 1

Chapter 1 includes an in-depth description of the Kardashians' background and history, including the foundations of *Keeping Up with the Kardashians*. Moreover, this initial chapter contains an analysis of show ratings and more importantly, economic scrutiny of their branding empire. This fiscal catalog includes: assessment of Kim Kardashian's popularity, analysis of "momager" Kris Jenner, consideration of product endorsement, and a survey of other means of revenue production. Lastly, this chapter also includes a clarification of narrative discourse analysis methodology.

Chapter 2

Through a theoretical framework of television studies, chapter 2 explores the first three dichotomies evident via the *Keeping Up with the Kardashians* narrative discourse analysis: family/business, intimacy/transgressions, and gender role contravention. These narratives connote certain American race, gender, and class notions as manifested through the Kardashians.

Family/Business

The first duality noticeable throughout the series is the contradiction between family and business. Historically, family and business have been intertwined; farmers relied on family to help harvest crops, and the family store was often passed from generation to generation. However, the ideal of individualism lauds the lone businessperson, succeeding not based on nepotism, but on the basis of his own entrepreneurial spirit and business acumen. While the Kardashians did begin their financial and celebrity trajectory with money inherited by Robert Kardashian, Sr., from his family's meatpacking business (Jenner, 2011), their celebrity status was largely self-engendered by momager Kris Jenner.

Kris Jenner had a low level of family fame and name recognition to build upon, namely through Robert Kardashian's participation in the O. J. Simpson murder trial and her subsequent husband's Olympic fame. However, by the 2007 debut of *Keeping Up with the Kardashians* Robert Kardashian had been dead for four years and Bruce Jenner's 1976 Olympic triumphs were long over. Kris parlayed Kim Kardashian's friendship with Paris Hilton (a hot celebrity in 2007) and sex tape with a D level celebrity (Ray J, brother of 90s singer Brandy) into a $60 million family income within three years. This achievement requires the aforementioned entrepreneurial spirit and business acumen, as well as participation of the Kardashians as a family, and conversely, the establishment of the Kardashian family as a corporation.

The conflation of the private sphere family life and the public sphere business world results in a profitable paradox for the Kardashians. The two realms are often in conflict with each other, providing drama and conflict for the television program. Cyclically, the two symbiotically feed the other; without conflict, the show couldn't exist, and without the show depicting the family, the commercial business aspect of the family wouldn't exist.

Intimacy/Transgression

Another way the Kardashians upset societal norms is via the dichotomy of family intimacy and transgressive closeness, which crosses normal boundaries. The family is extremely close, perhaps aspirationally intimate to viewers, despite their bickering. This conforms to the ideal of family as extremely important. However, the sexual nature of many interactions, often required for the partially business-oriented nature of some relationships, or indulged in for shock value, encroaches upon typical family relationships as depicted in media.

Other taboo sexual situations occur throughout the series, namely the sexualization of baby boomer age Kris and Bruce and the sexualization of pregnant Kourtney. As noted, the majority of sexual people on television are youthful; Kris and Bruce's sexual relationship upsets the norm. Moreover, while motherhood is a vaunted ideal throughout media, pregnant women are not usually depicted in a sexual manner, another taboo the Kardashians ignore.

As noted earlier, on television, whiteness is the racial benchmark (Wood, 2011) and black men are substantially underrepresented (Dixon and Azocar, 2006). Typically, reality TV exhibits racism by having only token participants (Pozner, 2010). Subverting these norms, on *Keeping Up with the Kardashians*, Khloé's husband Lamar is treated as an equal, with various plotlines dedicated to explaining his personality and background. The interracial component of their marriage, which in some parts of America is still controversial, is never mentioned and thus treated as a non-issue, as are Kim's various relationships with African-American men. The United States federally legalized interracial marriage only in 1967 (Loving v. Virginia, 1967).

Nevertheless, while the Kardashians may destabilize televised patriarchal, racial, and sexual norms, their embrace of dominant family ideals prevails. While their family may be interracial and Kourtney and Scott unmarried, as are Kim and Kanye West, the notion of the dream wedding and longing for children balance the more subversive elements in the program.

Gender Role Contravention

Throughout the series, to some extent the Kardashians support traditional gender role disparities, such as the dominant white male and subservient white woman (Pozner, 2010). However, overwhelmingly the Kardashians, namely Kris and Bruce, subvert the stereotypical gender norms typically depicted on television.

As Lotz noted, on television "women are now fortunate enough to be characterized in disparate and complex ways" (2006, p. 172). Contemporary televised women are illustrated in more complex fashions than their predecessors; diverse narratives are used to demonstrate various facets of personality, often aspects at odds with each other. This is true for Kris Jenner; she occupies dual, frequently contradictory roles of manager and mother.

While *Keeping Up with the Kardashians* may be family friendly, it truly challenges gender norms through its portrayal of a strong matriarchy. This investigation sheds light upon how conventional mediated messages may be evolving; not every televised familial relationship necessarily adheres to stale stereotypes of men and women's expected behavior. Women no longer need to be the Madonna or the whore; they can be both (or presumably neither). Moreover, men are no longer the inevitably dominant partner and family leader; out of the realm of reality TV, new paradigms are emerging.

Chapter 3

Chapter 3 continues the narrative study of the first seven seasons of *Keeping Up with the Kardashians*, particularly in regard to celebrity, elucidating the dualities of narcissism/celebrity, beauty/unhappiness, and sexual/conservative. Furthermore, three themes are highlighted and evaluated through the theoretical perspective of conspicuous consumption: materialism and consumerism, hard work, and perfect weddings.

Narcissism/Celebrity

Celebrity is continually asserted on the series as already attained (evidenced by invitations to red carpet events, fans, famous friends) and a goal toward which to strive (exemplified by the hard work of photo shoots and appearances). The other half of this dichotomy, narcissism, is spoken of in derogatory terms as a quality the sisters dislike. However, all of the Kardashian family members are narcissistic, caring intensely about their physical appearance, as illustrated throughout the series, and particularly substantiated by the number of plastic surgeries and cosmetic procedures underwent. Vanity is a family attribute, correlated to the materialism theme, in the acquisition of couture clothing and expensive accessories.

Moreover, it is the rare celebrity who can associate charity with his or her image, and not the attribute of self-centeredness. While the Kardashians often attempt to affiliate with a charity, such as Kim's embrace of the Dress for Success women's charity, this does not offset the myriad depictions of conceit. The unrelenting glare of the reality-TV camera, even with advantageous editing to engender a positive image, illustrates a primarily shallow existence based upon self-importance, self-satisfaction, and overall concern for self above all unrelated people.

Beauty/Unhappiness

The Kardashians paradoxically support and challenge the beauty status quo, while concurrently using it to their advantage. They pay lip service to the complexities of different body shapes, yet the discourse bolsters standard body norms, which typically results in family member unhappiness.

The sisters state clichés like encouraging viewers to "embrace your curves," ostensibly challenging beauty norms, yet the overall discourse stresses the need to be conventionally thin. While the sisters are curvaceous, they utilize exercise, plastic surgery, non-invasive cosmetic techniques, and appetite suppressants to try to reduce their waistlines. This contradicts their rare support of varied body images.

Kim Kardashian in particular is known for her outsized feminine shape, reminiscent of Marilyn Monroe's figure. On one occasion, she even has her behind x-rayed to prove she does not have buttock implants (S6, E3). While Kim is not fashion-model thin, she does have a slim waist and an hourglass figure. Her body does not look like an editorial fashion model's but rather a surgically enhanced *Playboy* bunny. This difficult-to-attain figure sets an almost unreachable goal for fans, and supports norms of sexuality and femininity.

While the Kardashians recognize standards of beauty, femininity, and sexuality, they also exploit them. Skeggs and Wood (2012) aver that through reality TV, women are using the "performances of their bodies, gestures, and language as themselves to their own material advantage" (p. 2). Kim Kardashian and her sisters exemplify this notion through the sexy good girl image. By combining the binary images prevalent throughout media, the good girl and the sex kitten, Kim portrays two values systems and gains a large audience, attracting fans of both images.

Moreover, the Kardashians utilize sexual appeal in calendars and magazine spreads, wearing bikinis, lingerie, or next to nothing. They use the established codes of what sexy means to earn money, appeal to fans, and build celebrity. Typically, men profit from women's sexuality; for example, *Playboy*, *Hustler* and other magazines of those ilk are famously owned by men, while the family-friendly version, *Sports Illustrated's* swimsuit issue, is part of the Time-Warner corporation. As of November 2012, Time-Warner's CEO was Jeffrey Bewkes, and of the five other senior executives, only one is a woman (Time Warner Senior Executives, 2012). A woman profiting from her own sexuality to the extent of the Kardashians is still unusual in American society.

Sexual/Conservative

The Kardashians are explicitly sexy, exploiting the sexual representation norm. Jhally (2006) notes conventionalized sexual imagery (e.g., high heels, slit skirts, and nudity) "draws us in and makes an ad attractive to us" (p. 172). The Kardashians utilize this for their own gain. While their silent bodies in advertisements and promotional materials draw the viewer in through blatant sexuality, the family benefiting from this is subversive. Men aren't exploiting the Kardashians; instead, the Kardashians are exploiting what audiences have been socialized to like. For example, the Kardashian Sears clothing line advertisements have been controversial; they often appear wearing minimal clothing, lingerie, or nothing at all. They objectify themselves, in order to profit financially, as well as amplify celebrity, which in turn grows fiscal success.

Moreover, Douglas (2010) asserts that media have transformed women's clamor for sexual equality into women's sexual objectification, which does not impart sexual power at all. This teaches girls to strive to become sex objects, catering to supposed male desires. Superficially, the Kardashian sisters may appear to characterize this "enlightened sexism," or the ostensibly attained gender parity while truly transmitting sexual stereotypes (Douglas, 2010). Indeed, their scantily clad illustrations in the media bolster the importance of stereotypes and may teach girls to rely upon their appearance. However, their ownership of the images and self-promotion for their own profit complicates enlightened sexism through consideration of economics. Whether viewers recognize this is unclear. However, the Kardashians are depicted in their television series as using their image for profit, through avidly participating in photoshoot decisions and choosing which photos will be published. They are never depicted as promiscuous or wild.

When the Kardashians sexualize themselves, they are contributing to Adrienne Rich's (1980/1994) conception of "compulsory heterosexuality," a societal norm assuming all women are heterosexual, in which heterosexuality is metaphorically (and in some instances, forcibly) obligatory for women. Rich also contends that sexual appeal is necessary for the majority of female occupations, and this helps perpetuate the overt and implicit sexist status quo. Moreover, male/female romantic love is an ideal permeated throughout media, establishing such relationships as a benchmark, which also helps to propagate the chauvinist heterosexist standard. The Kardashian sexualization of themselves simultaneously supports the objectification of women, making them complicit in "compulsory heterosexuality." However, because they are the ones accomplishing this for their own benefit, they mutate the status quo.

By co-opting their objectification and profiting from the perpetuation of the beauty industry and its norms, they simultaneously disrupt and maintain gender norms. The Kardashian image may be understood as emblematic of

McRobbie's (2009) post-feminism, in which working and earning money is hegemonically "offset by the emphasis on lifelong and carefully staged body maintenance as an imperative of feminine identity" (p. 63). However, the Kardashian business ventures complicate post-feminism: though hinged upon personal image betterment, from promoting Vela Shape to the Khroma makeup line, they directly benefit the family. While the Kardashians' success story may not have been intended to upset the institution of patriarchy, this is an unexpected byproduct of their entertainment industry achievement, even while maintaining seemingly unreachable beauty norms. While ultimately perhaps a societal detriment, the striving to attain problematic beauty norms benefits the Kardashian bottom line. Thus, the matriarchal family fashions their own singular version of feminism, built upon their successful self-exploitation.

Materialism and Perfect Weddings

Secondary themes within the series include that of materialism and perfect weddings. As Kim said in the first episode, "There's a lot of baggage that comes with us, but it's like Louis Vuitton luggage: You always want it." (S1, E1). This quote describes the conundrum of the Kardashians: they are immensely popular across varied media, often due to their entertaining baggage their conflicts may seem more interesting than other people's mundane issues due to their extremes: extreme wealth, large family, and excessive materialism. The quote also begins the casual referencing to name-brand expensive items which connote the family's wealth and status, and which may provide escapism for watchers, even while espousing materialism and consumerism.

The program endorsement of materialism, which doubtlessly in some part attracts an audience, also seems to promote fiscal irresponsibility during a recession. Nevertheless, the Kardashians follow in the tradition made customary by the programs of *Dallas, Dynasty,* and *Lifestyles of the Rich and Famous*, depicting the lives of the very wealthy, including their over-the-top extravagant weddings. Skeggs and Wood contend that reality TV "in maintaining and constantly reiterating normative standards" creates a "spectacularization of . . . excess" that "is used to generate audience attention (and ultimately advertisers)" (2012, p. 221). For audiences, this provides an aspirational model, a fantasy, and an escape from normal routines. For the Kardashians, their advocacy of materialism and consumerism plays into their own interests—in promotion of materialism they encourage audiences to buy their sponsors' products and their own merchandise. This relationship is indicative of the correlated nature of their intricate web of branding, celebrity, and commercialism.

Work Ethic

Another secondary theme within the series is work ethic. The family members repeatedly assert that they adhere to a serious work ethic and are consistently working with nary a break. Correspondingly, in the introduction of the sisters' book, *Kardashian Konfidential*, the sisters proclaim, "We work hard for what we have, and we believe in girl power" (2011, p. 7). Interrogating this claim reveals that the family members are truly referring to *time spent being themselves*, which they understand as work.

Hearn (2010), in her analysis of reality program *The Hills*, notes that "'being' is labor and produces financial value" for the "person characters, and for their producers, and for the MTV network" (pp. 61-61). This is true of the Kardashians as well; they regard hard work as time spent, not actually doing anything intellectually or physically demanding, but realizing what Andrejevic (2004) labeled "the work of being watched." Their labor is "being themselves" for the cameras, the time spent in hair and makeup, and then recording their ostensibly unscripted lives. However, unlike the vast majority of reality television participants, the Kardashians themselves benefit from their portrayal as producers and creators of the program and ancillary products, complicating Andrejevic's analysis.

Chapter 4

Chapter 4 investigates the social media confluence of celebrity, new media, and commerce via narrative analyses of Kim Kardashian's Twitter feed and blog, exploring how the Kardashian family members' social media usage affects their celebrity, branding, and finances. The Twitter analysis found narratives of personal tidbits, lifestyle, interaction with fans, interaction with celebrities, encouraging traffic to website, and promotional/publicity. Within Kim's blog, the study determined the following narratives existed: family and authenticity, celebrity, business, behind the scenes, beauty, social media, and the amalgamated category of family/business/celebrity.

The Kardashians strategically use social media to interweave and bolster celebrity, branding, and finances. As Jenkins (1998) noted, multi-platform interactivity facilitates online meaning making. Their social media participation amplifies celebrity by various means, including providing a fan connection and thus increased fan loyalty, unifies their brand into a single saleable image, and subsequently augments revenue in a complex fashion.

A primary facet of the Kardashians social media utilization is the use of the same content across multiple platforms, guaranteeing that content reaches users of varied media. For example, Kim's Facebook and Twitter feeds both may feature a link to Kim's most recent blog post, which then links back to those social media, or may include a link to one of her sister's social media outlets. In this way, Kim creates a feedback loop amongst social media portals, sending users around through a maze of Kardashian media. Alternately, if a person only uses Twitter, he or she receives the message that a new blog post exists. In another example, a blog post may highlight action that will appear on that night's episode of *Keeping Up with the Kardashians* via a link to a YouTube trailer. Similarly, Kim's tweets entreat viewers to watch the shows, check out her blog, and buy products she endorses or creates.

By connecting the various outlets and featuring the same content on multiple platforms, the Kardashians establish and add to their coherent identity, creating a solidified, integrated celebrity brand that fans can easily respond to in multiple fashions. Fans can like a Facebook post, retweet a Tweet, link to a YouTube video (or other online media), and in all these media, reply directly to the Kardashian family or to other fans. This interactivity creates a fan group collective identity (McClain, 2011) and promotes brand loyalty (Jenkins, 2006). Moreover, social media permits a means to generate and refine the Kardashian persona comprised of celebrity status, authentic voice, and family involvement. This image blends together the values of hard work and materialism, family collectivity and individualism, promotion and sincerity, and entrepreneurialism and dependence upon fans. This dynamic mix is an amalgamation to which fans clearly respond, literally on social media, and figuratively through purchasing products.

The sales push is both overt and implied throughout the Kardashian social media. Several categories of tweets and blog posts are direct sales pitches, uncomplicated and easy to understand. Other sales pitches are more insinuated, masked as posts lauding a sister's work, or ostensibly about family bonding time. However, whenever a product is mentioned, the tweet or post serves to surreptitiously remind audiences about a particular product. Indeed, whenever a product is not outwardly related to the Kardashian empire of merchandise, an outside company pays for that product placement. This wouldn't be possible without the rapt audience drawn by the social-media-refined celebrity and seemingly authentic persona. The sisters themselves are a branded product, ready for social media consumption through pictures, written words, videos, and links. The web of social media and television exposure, combined with the carefully crafted status updates engendering authentic/celebrity, draws fan eyeballs, which in turn strengthens finances in terms of actual revenue of purchased items, the amount able to charged for endorsements, better television deals, and myriad new merchandise and media opportunities.

In sum, Kim Kardashian's social media use confirms her celebrity, aids in authenticity creation, links Kim to her fan community as well as promotes its vitality, sells her products, and sustains the theme of materialism. Moreover, reiteration of the same material throughout social media bolsters the Kardashian identity, engenders a comprehensible brand, and establishes a marketable image.

Chapter 5

Chapter 5 is an analysis of 2011 Kardashian press coverage. Narratives found include: body image, family relationships, social media, branding and business, popularity, and the marriage and divorce of Kim Kardashian and Kris Humphries. This last study reveals contemporary reactions to the family and their celebrity, underlying themes throughout reporting, and the role journalism plays in constructing and reflecting societal standards. This analysis revealed the mainstream journalists' injurious opinions of the family. While the press decries the Kardashian popularity, overall they neglect to point out the hegemonic support of capitalistic ideals and cultural norms apparent in the family's media presence. Interestingly, this study also found that as a consequence of the Kardashian popularity, the term Kardashian is being used as a synecdoche for all reality TV stars.

People, like journalists, greatly detest the Kardashians for a variety of reasons, but one motivation for this may be the Kardashians' apparent achievement of the American dream *without the visible hard work required for it* and the subsequent flaunting of their wealth. The Kardashians appear to have it all: a large loving family in good health, as well as beauty, fame, and money. The press repeatedly reiterates that they have attained all of this by doing nothing of merit, by simply filming their glamorous lives. This is in direct contrast to the family's assertion of constant hard work. While there may be a disconnect between the press's perception of work and the family's, the fact remains that according to the reporters, the Kardashians are famous for no reason at all. Thus, they do not warrant the accomplishment of the American dream. Moreover, the Kardashians brandish their apparently unearned wealth on television and across various media, which may have been particularly odious during an economic recession such as the one that began in 2008.

The Kardashians are undoubtedly wealthy. However, they are nouveau riche, or new money, which is traditionally looked down upon in American society. While this may seem to be an outdated concept in the era of famous-for-fifteen-minutes reality TV stars, socially prominent blue-bloods like the Kennedys are still vaunted in American society. Similarly, in 2011 Americans renewed their fascination with the Windsor family of Britain, namely Prince William, Duchess Catherine, and Prince Harry. This indicates a still present American class system, not only based upon wealth and property holdings, but also based upon bloodlines. In contrast to old-money American nobility, the Kardashians are California based, and only a few generations removed from the old country of Armenia. Robert Kardashian's paternal grandparents immigrated to America in 1913, avoiding the 1915 Armenian Genocide by the Turkish (Harvey, 2012). Their wealth does not buy them class.

Another reason for journalists' dislike of the Kardashians may be that they disrupt institutional norms still existent in American society, like patriarchy, marriage, and women's exploitation, rather than exploiting sexuality for their own gain. Sexism and classism may also be a factor in the censure of the Kardashians. While women are often authoritative and powerful in media depictions, this is not reflected in off-screen reality (Douglas, 2010). A 2010 report by the U.S. Census Bureau averred that women earn 77 percent of mens' yearly salary. Similarly, a woman with the same level of education as a man will earn approximately $1.2 million less than him over the course of her lifetime (Corbett and Hill, 2012). Not only do women earn less money, but institutional sexism still exists within governmental and cultural institutions, as well as in beliefs that women are of a lesser intellect and cannot perform the same duties as men. While the 2012 elections added a record-setting number of women to Congress, the Senate includes only twenty female members out of 100, while the House of Representatives counts seventy-eight women of 435 members (Camia, 2013). This speaks to the influence of sexism that still exists today. The Kardashians, a strong matriarchy, are recipients of this sexism. They are women who created celebrity from barely any name recognition, and who run multiple successful companies in many different areas of business. In particular, Kris Jenner could be lauded for her entrepreneurial efforts, instead of lampooned in the press for fostering her daughters' careers. A comparable male successful businessperson may be Donald Trump. Trump, while a successful independent entrepreneur, inherited the beginnings of his fortune, a fact not often mentioned by journalists. Through his reality-competition series *The Apprentice*, Trump also participates in reality television, although isn't denigrated in the press for it. Trump also doesn't exploit his sexuality for profit; another possible reason mainstream media disparages the Kardashians. Even while maintaining widely ridiculed political opinions, Trump merits more respect and less defamation in the press than the Kardashians.

Overall, the press coverage indicates that while the Kardashians often challenge norms on their television shows, the popular press, and by extension American society, is seemingly not ready for this change. Institutional sexism and classism are still prevalent. While some deplore the Kardashians' reality TV-induced fame, exploitation of sexual norms, and the ostensible preying upon young audience naivety in response to social media and sexual images, the popularity of the Kardashians indicate that audiences may agree with them and their values. In sum, despite their popularity, the denigration faced by the Kardashians indicates that America is not ready for a strong matriarchy, sexual exploitation of female bodies for their owners' profit, and extremely successful female entrepreneurs.

COMMODIFICATION OF FAMILY INTO CELEBRITY, BRAND, AND REVENUE

Using emotions to provide not just authenticity (McClain, 2011) but also profits follows Illouz's (2007) concept of intimacy as a commodity. Emotions and capitalism are connected, as Illouz contends, and the Kardashians exemplify this. Their self-made illustrations of their everyday existence necessarily include emotional highs and lows. As audience members profess to watch for moments of what they consider to be true emotions (Hill, 2005) the Kardashians must exhibit joy, sorrow, and anger in order to attract and appease consumers. The more people in their audience, the more seasons *Keeping Up with the Kardashians* may run, the more spin-offs can be developed, and the more products they can endorse and create. Thus, the Kardashians commodify their own portrayed emotions through mediated discourse.

Discourse produces fame (Turner, 2004). As such, the Kardashians' celebrity was created and is maintained through discourse. Their fame, engendered by reality TV and social media, begets more media attention, which cyclically produces more fame. Concurrently, their fame operates as a social function (Hermes, 1995; Turner, 2004; Turner, Bonner, and Marshall, 2000), connoting culturally recognizable meanings, alternately bolstering and transforming them. Finally, the Kardashians function as a commodity, endorsing materialism, and as a brand, providing a salable image.

The Kardashians commodify their family as well. Even the births of Kourtney's two children were featured on the show and shared with a nationwide audience, in part to attract viewers and new endorsements. By recording and televising Mason and Penelope's births, the series capitalized upon and monetized the intimate nature of the show and the viewers' perceived intimate relationship with the family. One view of this overt commodification of a natural, family-bonding event is as a crass repurposing of family milestone; another perspective positions televising the births as merely sharing family occasions with the larger, family-like community audience. Regardless, depicting the births on TV is a normal progression of the no-holds-barred personal nature of the Kardashian series; utilizing all life events as fodder for the show, commodifying their lives in expectation of fiscal benefits.

In a contradiction of Kardashian precedent, in December of 2012, Kim and Kanye West announced the imminent birth of their child at a West concert. The cavalier nature of this announcement contradicts the typical planned nature of the Kardashian media and life events. Not only potentially missing out on a payday connected to the announcement, Kim reportedly has already turned down a \$3 million offer for the first baby pictures and says infant West will not participate on *Keeping Up with the Kardashians* (Stoeffel, 2013). However, if Kim were to follow her sister Kourtney's example in commodifying her pregnancy, birth, and newborn, she stands to greatly financially benefit. Whether Kim's relationship with Kanye will revise her media utilization truly remains to be seen. She is contractually obligated to participate in future seasons of the series; moreover, her family, brand, and celebrity will suffer without her media presence.

Overall, the Kardashian media are commercials for perfumes, clothing, other media, and whatever product the Kardashians are selling. Not only do the shows promote consumerism and materialism, but also the idea of selling yourself. The conflation of business and personal reduces the value of a person to his or her selling potential.

KEEPING UP THE KARDASHIAN BRAND: CELEBRITY, MATERIALISM, AND SEXUALITY

The Kardashians are a paradigm of new media and old media convergence, highlighting the confluence of branding, commerce, celebrity, and sexuality. The Kardashians exemplify the American dream through their entrepreneurial nature and success, and demonstrate a new element of the American dream, celebrity, which they maintain through seemingly intimate social media fan relationships. Their branding and celebrity empire would not exist without smart use of social media. Their usage is an exemplar of how to buttress popularity, extend celebrity, and associate image and products. The Kardashians are a prototype of how social media usage can be used to attain the American dream of success.

The Kardashians also represent extremes of American culture, exulting traditional values of family, love, fidelity and newer values of celebrity, narcissism, and materialism. They may strike a chord with some audience members by portraying certain old-fashioned values, as well as younger viewers by referencing the embrace of social media, interracial romance, and girl power. However, all of the dualities, themes, and values function to naturalize overt sexuality, celebrity, materialism, and capitalism. Conspicuous consumption is visible through the portrayed materialism evident across media.

While superficially the shows may connote beauty and body ideals through the sisters' bodies, more complex notions lie within the polished image. Societal norms are not simple or easily definable, on-screen or off-screen. Undeniably, media analysis helps elucidate contemporary society. The Kardashians embody many conflicting values; doubtlessly these all influence and mimic the world we live in. The ideas and values depicted by the shows and the Kardashians themselves are diverse and multilayered: traditional and contemporary, sexual and smart, hardworking and easily attainable, and close-knit and too close for comfort. The Kardashians personify the contradictions present within all people; however, theirs play out on a national stage and are exploited for profit. This book explains what the Kardashian family, complete with its contradictions and ideals, epitomizes in contemporary American culture; ideals of loyalty and love, wealth and consumerism, sexuality and fidelity, and fame and family.

The Kardashians successfully monetize themselves, social media, television series, celebrity, and their fans, transforming those components into a flourishing and lucrative brand. All of these factors are intricately related and sustain each other. The various elements of the complex web symbiotically rely upon each other to create the Kardashian brand identity of femininity, family, fame, and fortune. Moreover, the action of effectively commodifying the family via multiple media platforms links materialism, social identity, and celebrity, ultimately upholding a governing American ideology: capitalism.

Bibliography

Ahmad, A. (2010). Is Twitter a useful tool for journalists? *Journal of Media Practice, 11* (2), 145-155.

Andrejevic, M. (2004). *Reality TV: The work of being watched.* New York: Rowman & Littlefield Publishers, Inc.

Andrejevic, M. (2011). Social network exploitation. In Z. Papacharissi (Ed.), *A networked self: Identity, community, and culture on social network sites* (pp. 82-101). New York: Routledge.

Apatoff, A. (2011, December 26). Kylie and Kendall Jenner Are the Newest Celeb Jewelry Designers. *People Magazine.* Retrieved from http://stylenews.peoplestylewatch.com/2011/12/26/kylie-and-kendall-jenner-newest-celeb-jewelry-designers/.

Arvidsson, A. (2007). Creative class or administrative class? On advertising and the "underground." *Ephemera, 1.*

Bagwell, L. & Bernheim, D. (1996). Veblen effects in a theory of conspicuous consumption. *American Economic Review, 86* (3), 349-373.

Bal, M. (2009). *Narratology* (3rd. ed.). Buffalo, New York: University of Toronto Press.

Banks, J. and Humphreys, S. (2008). The labour of user co-creators. *Convergence, 14* (4), 201-418.

Bardon, N. (2011, April 1). Khloe: Fat days bring me down. *The Sun.* Retrieved from the Newspapers Plus database.

Barthes, R. (1977). Introduction to the structural image of the narrative. In *Image, music text* (79-124). New York: Hill and Wang.

Berger, A. (1996). *Narratives in popular culture, media, and everyday life.* Beverly Hills, CA: Sage Publications.

Bird, E. and Dardenne, R. (1988). Myth, chronicle, and story: Exploring the narrative qualities of news. In J. Carey (ed.), *Media, myths, and narrative* (67-86). Beverly Hills, CA: Sage Publications.

Bodgas, M. (2011, April 27). The average diamond engagement ring carat weight is. . . (and where does yours fall?). *Glamour.com.* Retrieved from http://www.glamour.com/weddings/blogs/save-the-date/2011/04/the-average-diamond-engagement.html#ixzz23XgVGQZs.

Boldface Licensing + Branding announces Khroma Beauty by Kourtney, Kim and Khloe Kardashian (2012, June 7). [Press release]. Retrieved from http://www.hawaiinewsnow.com/story/18731053/boldface-licensing-branding-announces-khroma-beauty-by-kourtney-kim-and-khloe-kardashian.

Boorstin, D. (1961/1992). *The image.* New York: Vintage Books.

Bosman, J. (2011, June 1). In their own words? Maybe. *The New York Times*. Retrieved from http://www.nytimes.com/2011/06/02/fashion/noticed-celebrity-books-and-ghostwriters. html.

Braudy, L. (1997). *The frenzy of renown*. New York: Vintage Books.

Brenoff, A. (2008, December 27). Kardashian home in Hidden Hills for sale at $3,395,000. *Los Angeles Times*. Retrieved from http://www.latimes.com/features/la-hm-hotprop272008dec27,0,1930552,full.story.

Bridgeman, D. (2007). Time and space. In D. Herman (Ed.), *The Cambridge companion to narrative* (pp. 52-65). New York: Cambridge University Press.

Brooker, W. (2002). Overflow and audience. In W. Brooker and D. Jermyn (Eds.), *The Audience studies reader* (pp. 322-333). London: Routledge.

Brooks, D. and Hebert, L. (2006). Gender, race, and media representation. In B. Dow and J.T. Wood (Eds.), *Handbook of Gender and Communication* (pp. 297-317). Thousand Oaks, CA: Sage.

Brunsdon, C., D'Acci, J. & Spigel, L. (1997). Introduction. In C. Brunsdon, J. D'Acci, & L. Spigel (Eds.), *Feminist television criticism* (pp. 1-19). Oxford: Clarendon Press.

Burling, S. (2011, February 21). Chasing shifting body ideals: Homework still a must. *The Philadelphia Inquirer*. Retrieved from the Newspapers Plus database.

Burns, S. (2011, July 10). Hey homies, you're earning me £30,000 a tweet. *Mail on Sunday*. Retrieved from the Newspapers Plus database.

Butler, J. (2006). *Television: Critical methods and applications (3rd ed.)*. Mahwah, NJ: Lawrence Erlbaum Assoc.

Cain, J., Scott, D., and Smith, K. (2010). Use of social media by residency program directors for resident selection. *Journal of Health-System Pharmacy, 67* (19), 1635-1639.

Camia, C. (2013, January 4). Record number of women in Congress. *USA Today*. p. 4A.

Carmichael, K. (2009). Capital investment. *American Journalism Review, 31* (5), 8-9.

Casserly, (2012, May 16). Khloe Kardashian Odom: The dark horse of TV's most famous family. *Forbes.com*. Retrieved from http://www.forbes.com/sites/meghancasserly/2012/05/16/khloe-kardashian-odom-celebrity-100-dark-horse/2/.

Chang, B. (2011, October 30). Role-playing each day. *The New York Times*. Retrieved from the Newspapers Plus database.

Chayko, M. (2002). *Connecting: How we form social bonds and communities in the Internet age*. Albany, NY: SUNY Press.

Chayko, M. (2008). *Portable communities: The social dynamics of online and mobile connectedness*. Albany, NY: SUNY Press.

Clark, C. (2011, August 20). Kardashian, Humphries wed in glittery affair. *USA Today*. Retrieved September 11, 2013, from http://usatoday30.usatoday.com/life/people/2011-08-20-Kim-Kardashian-gets-married_n.htm.

Clark, G. (2009). Environmental Twitter. *Environment, 51* (5), 5-7.

Cohen, N. (2008). The valorization of surveillance: Towards a political economy of Facebook. *Democratic Communiqué, 22* (1), 5-22.

Cohen, S. (2011, August 20). Kim's wedding is big business for the Kardashians. *The Associated Press*. Retrieved from the Newspapers Plus database.

Corbett, C. and Hill, C. (2012). *Graduating to a pay gap: The earnings of women and men one year after college graduation*. Washington, DC: American Association of University Women.

Corner, J. (2002). "Performing the Real: Documentary Diversions." *Television & New Media, 3* (3), 255-269.

Coyle, J. (2011, March 7). Behind Charlie Sheen's tweet lies a new world of social media advertising. *The Canadian Press*. Retrieved from the Newspapers Plus database.

Currid-Halkett, E. (2010). *Starstruck: The business of celebrity*. New York: Faber and Faber, Inc.

Curtain, M. & Shattuc, J. (2009). *The American television industry*. New York: Palgrave Macmillan.

Curnutt, H. (2009). A fan crashing the party: Exploring reality-celebrity in MTV's Real World franchise. *Television & New Media, 10*, 251-266.

de Bertodano, H. (2011, June 25). The woman who mistook her life for a brand. *The Times (United Kingdom)*. Retrieved from the Newspapers Plus database.

de Cordova, R. (1990). *Picture personalities: The emergence of the star system in America.* Champaign, IL: University of Illinois Press.

de Moraes, L. (2011, November 4). Keeping up with E!'s defense of its Kardashian wedding coverage. *The Washington Post*. Retrieved from the Newspapers Plus database.

Derakhshani, T. (2011, January 4). Sideshow column. *The Philadelphia Inquirer.* Retrieved from the Newspapers Plus database.

Deuze, M. (2007). Convergence culture in the creative industries. *International Journal of Cultural Studies, 10* (2), 243-266.

Devlin, R. (2011, January 5). Boring parts of life are boring . . . no matter who does them. *The Courier Mail (Australia)*. Retrieved from the Newspapers Plus database.

Ding, K. (2011, January 6). Lamar Odom's reality endeavor a well-deserved endeavor. *The Orange County Register.* Retrieved from the Newspapers Plus database.

Dixon, T. and Azocar, C. (2006). The representation of juvenile offenders by race on Los Angeles area television news. *Howard Journal of Communication, 17*, pp. 143-161.

Domjen, B. and Moran, J. (2011, January 2). No size-zero tolerance as curves make a come-back. *The Sunday Telegraph (Sydney)*. Retrieved from the Newspapers Plus database.

Donvan, J. (2011, October 31.) Love and the bottom line. [Television Broadcast]. *Nightline.* New York: ABC. Transcript retrieved from the Newspapers Plus database.

Douglas, S. (2010). *The rise of enlightened sexism.* New York: St. Martin's Griffin.

Dovey, J. (2000). *Freakshow: First person media and factual television.* London: Pluto.

Dow, B. (2006). Introduction: Gender and communication in mediated contexts. In B. Dow & J. Wood (Eds.), *The Sage Handbook of gender and communication* (pp. 263-273). Thousand Oaks, CA: Sage.

Dugan, L. (2011, February 15). *As Twitter grows, its users grow older.* Retrieved from http://www.mediabistro.com/alltwitter/as-twitter-grows-its-users-grow-older_b3398.

Dyer, R. (1986/2004). *Heavenly bodies: Film stars and society.* (2nd ed.). New York: Routledge.

E! Entertainment. (2012, May 21). E!'s "Keeping Up with the Kardashians" season premiere delivers nearly 3 million total viewers, besting previous season premiere by +16% [Press release]. Retrieved from http://www.nbcumv.com/mediavillage/networks/eentertainment/keepingupwiththekardashians/pressreleases?pr=contents/press-releases/2012/05/21/eskeepingupwith1337627946824.xml.

Ellis, J. (1992). *Visible fictions: Cinema, television, video.* London: Routledge.

Esmalian, A. (2010, October 13). Lamar Odom's new manager: Mama Kris Jenner. *Holly Scoop.* Retrieved from http://www.hollyscoop.com/lamar-odom/lamar-odoms-new-manager-mama-kris-jenner_25399.aspx.

Facebook newsroom. (2012, August 27). Retrieved from http://newsroom.fb.com/content/default.aspx?NewsAreaId=22.

Farhi, P. (2009). The Twitter explosion. *American Journalism Review, 31* (3), 26-31.

Fernandez, S. (2011, September 9). E!'s "Keeping Up with the Kardashians" hits ratings high. *Hollywood Reporter.* Retrieved from http://www.hollywoodreporter.com/live-feed/es-keeping-up-kardashians-hits-231695.

Feuer, J. (1986). "Narrative Form in American Network Television." In C. MacCabe (Ed.), *High Theory/Low Culture* (pp. 101–114). Manchester: Manchester University Press.

Finlayson, A. (2012, June 28). Kendall and Kylie Jenner set to write a fantasy novel. *US Weekly*. Retrieved from http://www.usmagazine.com/entertainment/news/Kendall-and-kylie-jenner-set-to-write-a-fantasy-novel2012286#ixzz1zBxxjb6P.

Fiske, J. (1987). *Television culture.* New York: Methuen.

Fiske, J. (1989). *Reading the popular.* New York: Routledge.

Fiske, J. (2000). The codes of television. In P. Marris and S. Thornham (eds.), *Media Studies: A reader* (220-30). New York: New York University Press.

Fitzgerald, B. (2012). Instagram's most popular users: The 15 most-followed celebs. *The Huffington Post.* Retrieved from http://www.huffingtonpost.com/2012/08/24/instagram-most-popular-users_n_1827904.html#slide=1379787.

Foster, Z. (2011, January 9). Talents to really sing about. *The Sunday Telegraph (Australia).* Retrieved from the Newspapers Plus database.

Friedman, J. (2002). Introduction. In J. Friedman (ed.), *Reality squared* (1–22). New Brunswick, NJ: Rutgers University Press.

Gamson, J. (1994). *Claims to fame: Celebrity in contemporary America.* Berkeley, CA: University of California Press.

Giles, D. (2000). *Illusions of immortality: A Psychology of fame and celebrity.* New York: St. Martin's Press.

Gill, R. (2008). Empowerment/sexism: Figuring female sexual agency in contemporary advertising. *Feminism & Psychology, 18,* 35-60.

Gilpin, D. (2011). Working the twittersphere: Microblogging as professional identity construction. In Z. Papacharissi (Ed.), *A networked self: Identity, community, and culture on social network sites* (pp. 232-250). New York: Routledge.

Goffman, E. (1959). *The presentation of self in everyday life.* Garden City, NY: Doubleday & Co.

Goldberg, D. (2011, December 14). From Fergie to Snooki to Britney, celebs earn top dollars for Las Vegas New Year's Eve appearances. *The Las Vegas Sun.* Retrieved from the Newspapers Plus database.

Goldberg, S. (2011, November 1). Kim Kardashian, Kris Humphries: Are you surprised? *CNN.* Retrieved from http://www.cnn.com/2011/11/01/showbiz/celebrity-news-gossip/kim-kardashian-kris-humphries-divorce/index.html.

Gordon, J. (2011, January 4). Technology-influenced ways to drop pounds. *St. Joseph News-Press (MO).* Retrieved from the Newspapers Plus database.

Gormish, R. (2012, August 24). Kim Kardashian announces "Kardashian Kurves" for plus sized women. *Examiner.com.* Retrieved from http://www.examiner.com/article/kim-kardashian-announces-kardashian-kurves-for-plus-sized-women.

Gramsci, A. (1971). *Selections from the prison notebooks of Antonio Gramsci.* New York: International Publishers Co.

Gray, J. (2009). Cinderella burps: Gender, performativity, and the dating show. In S. Murray and L. Ouellette (eds.), *Reality TV: Remaking television culture (2nd ed.)* (pp. 260-277). New York: New York University Press.

Greysen, S. R., Kind, T., and Chretien, K. (2010). Online professionalism and the mirror of social media. *Journal of General Internal Medicine, 25* (11), 1227-1229.

Hall, A. (2009). Perceptions of the authenticity of reality programs and their relationships to audience involvement, enjoyment, and perceived learning. *Journal of Broadcasting & Electronic Media, 53*(4), 515-531.

Hall, S. (1980/1991). Encoding/decoding. In S. Hall, D. Hobson, A. Lowe, & P. Willis (Eds.), *Culture, media, language: Working papers in cultural studies, 1972-1979* (pp. 128-138). New York: Routledge.

Hammer, A.J. (Writer). (2011a, May 26). Scotty McCreery and Lauren Alaina in Love?; The big Kim Kardashian ring debate; New development on the Arnold Schwarzenegger cheating scandal; Lindsay Lohan on house arrest; The "American Idol" star showdowns [Television series episode]. *Showbiz Tonight.* Atlanta: CNN. Transcript retrieved from the Newspapers Plus database.

Hammer, A.J., Winter, K. and Moos, J. (Writers). (2011, May 11). Arnold Schwarzenegger's dramatic revelations about Maria Shriver; Kim Kardashian's brand-new confessions about getting married; Bristol Palin's new face; Will Smith, a bad neighbor? [Television Broadcast]. *Showbiz Tonight.* Atlanta: CNN. Transcript retrieved from the Newspapers Plus database.

Harrison, K. (2008). Adolescent body image and eating in the media: Trends and implications for adolescent health. In P.E. Jamieson & D. Romer (Eds.), *The changing portrayals of adolescents in the media since 1950* (p. 165-197). New York: Oxford University Press.

Harvey, O. (2012, March 16). Kim Kardashian is keeping up with the Armenians. The Sun. Retrieved from http://www.thesun.co.uk/sol/homepage/features/3973452/Kim-Kardashian-is-keeping-up-with-the-Armenians.html.

Hawn, C. (2009). Take two aspirin and tweet me in the morning: How Twitter, Facebook, and other social media are reshaping health care. *Health Affairs, 28* (2), 361-368.

Hearn, A. (2010). Reality television and the limits of immaterial labor. *Triple C, 8* (1), 60-76.

Herman, D. (2007). Introduction. In D. Herman (Ed.), *The Cambridge companion to narrative* (pp. 3-21). New York: Cambridge University Press.

Herman, L. & Vervaeck, B. (2007). Ideology. In D. Herman (Ed.), *The Cambridge companion to narrative* (pp. 217-230). New York: Cambridge University Press.

Hermes, J. (1995). *Reading women's magazines: An analysis of everyday media use.* Cambridge: Polity.

Hermes, J. (1999). Media figures in identity construction. In P. Alasuutari (Ed.), *Rethinking the media audience: The new agenda* (pp. 69-85). London: Sage.

Herring, S. (Ed.). (1996). *Computer-mediated communication: Linguistic, social, and cross-cultural perspectives.* Amsterdam: John Benjamins.

Hill, A. (2005). *Reality TV: Audiences and popular factual television.* New York: Routledge.

Hill, A. (2007). *Big Brother*: The real audience. In H. Newcomb (Ed.), *Television: The critical view (7th ed)* (pp. 471-485). New York: Oxford University Press.

Holmes, S. (2004). "All you've got to worry about is the task, having a cup of tea, and doing a bit of sunbathing": Approaching celebrity in *Big Brother*. In S. Holmes, & D. Jermyn (Eds.), *Understanding reality television* (pp. 111-135). New York: Routledge.

Holtzman, L. (2000). *Media Messages: What Film, Television, and Popular Music Teach Us about Race, Class, Gender, and Sexual Orientation.* Armonk, NY: M. E. Sharpe, Inc.

Horovitz, B. (2011, February 4). Handing off to multi-media. *USA Today*. Retrieved from the Newspapers Plus database.

Hughes, S. (2011, May 25). Kim Kardashian given 20.5-carat ring by Kris Humphries: Which celeb had the biggest ring? *The Washington Post*. Retrieved from http://www.washingtonpost.com/blogs/celebritology/post/kim-kardashian-given-205-carat-ring-by-kris-humphries-which-celeb-had-the-biggest-ring/2011/05/25/AGDUJOBH_blog.html.

Illouz, E. (2007). *Cold intimacies: The making of emotional capitalism.* Cambridge: Polity Press.

Inside Track. (2011, January 24). *Boston Herald.* Retrieved from the Newspapers Plus database.

Jenkins, B. (2011, January 12). Lakers' soap opera in full swoon. *San Francisco Chronicle.* Retrieved from the Newspapers Plus database.

Jenkins, H. (1998). *The poachers and the stormtroopers: Cultural convergence in the digital age.* Retrieved from http://web.mit.edu/cms/People/henry3/pub/stormtroopers.htm.

Jenkins, H. (1992). *Textual poachers: Television fans and participatory culture.* Routledge: New York.

Jenkins, H. (2006). *Convergence culture: Where old and new media collide.* New York: New York University Press.

Jenner, K. (2011). *Kris Jenner and all things Kardashian.* New York: Gallery Books.

Jensen, J. (2010, September 3). Naked ambition. *Entertainment Weekly, 1118*, 42-46.

Jhally, S. (2006). *The spectacle of accumulation: Essays in culture, media, and politics.* New York: Peter Lang.

Jhally, S. & Katz, J. (2001, Winter). Big trouble, little pond: Reflections on the meaning of the campus pond rapes. *Umass*, pp. 26-31.

Jones, G., Schieffelin, B., & Smith, R. (2011). When friends who talk together stalk together: Online gossip as meta-communication (pp. 26-47). In C. Thurlow & K. Mroczek (Eds.), *Digital discourse*. New York: Oxford University Press.

Juzwiak, R. (2011, August 19). A world without the Kardashians. *The Washington Post*. Retrieved from the Newspapers Plus database.

Kakutani, M. (2011, September 11). Outdone by reality. *The New York Times*. Retrieved from the Newspapers Plus database.

Kardashian, Kim, Kardashian, Kourtney, and Kardashian, Khloe. (2010). *Kardashian Konfidential*. New York: St. Martin's Press.

Kim Kardashian's ShoeDazzle gets $40 million financing (May 17, 2011). L.A. Biz, Retrieved from http://www.bizjournals.com/losangeles/news/2011/05/17/kim-kardashians-shoedazzle-gets-40-m.html.

Kim says she's no sex symbol. (2011, January 5). *The Gold Coast Bulletin*. Retrieved from the Newspapers Plus database.

Kellner, D. (1995). *Media culture: Cultural studies, identity, and politics between modern and postmodern*. New York: Routledge.

Kendall, L. (2002). *Hanging out in the virtual pub: Masculinities and relationships online*. Berkeley: University of California Press.

Khloe Kardashian loses her $850,000 engagement ring! (2010, September 2). *US Weekly*. Retrieved from http://www.usmagazine.com/entertainment/news/khloe-kardashian-loses-her-engagement-ring-201029.

Kompare, D. (2009). Extraordinarily ordinary*: The Osbournes* as "An American family." In S. Murray and L. Ouellette (eds.), *Reality TV: Remaking television culture (2 nd ed.)* (pp. 100–119). New York: New York University Press.

Kress, G. & van Leeuwen, T. (2006). Digital literacy and participation in online social networking spaces. In C. Lankshear & M. Knobel (Eds.), *Digital literacies* (pp. 249-278). New York: Peter Lang.

Lang, A. (2011, July 15). Los Angeles is using celebrities to plead with drivers to stay off the highway this weekend. Canada: CBC Television. Transcript retrieved from the Newspapers Plus database.

Langer, J. (1981). TV's personality system. *Media, Culture and Society, 4*, 351–65.

Lee, C. (2011). Status updates on Facebook: Texts and practices (pp. 110-128). In C. Thurlow & K. Mroczek (Eds.), *Digital discourse*. New York: Oxford University Press.

Lee, E., Newton, C. and Temple, J. (2011, January 2). Facebook knocks Google off top of the list of most-visited sites. *San Francisco Chronicle*. Retrieved from the Newspapers Plus database.

Lenhart, A. & Fox, S. (2006). *Bloggers: A portrait of the Internet's new storytellers*. Washington, DC: Pew Research Center's Internet & American Life Project.

Lenihan, A. (2011). "Join our community of translators': Language ideologies and/in Facebook (pp. 48-64). In C. Thurlow & K. Mroczek (Eds.), *Digital discourse*. New York: Oxford University Press.

Leonhardt, D. (March 24, 2011). A better way to measure Twitter influence. *The New York Times*. Retrieved from http://6thfloor.blogs.nytimes.com/2011/03/24/a-better-way-to-measure-twitter-influence/

Levin, D. and Kilbourne, J. (2008). *So sexy, so soon*. New York: Ballantine.

Levine, S. (2012, January 30). 'Kourtney & Kim' finale a hit for E! *Variety.com*. Retrieved September 11, 2013 from http://variety.com/2012/tv/news/kourtney-kim-finale-a-hit-for-e-1118049475/.

Lotz, A. (2006). *Redesigning women: television after the network era*. Urbana: University of Illinois Press.

Loving v. Virginia. 388 U.S. 1. number U.S. (1967). Retrieved December 4, 2012 from http://caselaw.lp.findlaw.com/scripts/getcase.pl?court=US&vol=388&invol=1.

Lowenthal, L. (1961). *Literature, popular culture, and society*. Englewood Cliffs, NJ: Prentice-Hall.

Lundy, L. Ruth, A. & Park, T. (2008). Simply irresistible: Reality TV consumption patterns. *Communication Quarterly, 56*, 208-225.

Magrath, A. (2011, January 26). The church of Kardashians: Reality star Kim reveals to Piers Morgan that she funds church founded by her mother. *The Daily Mail*. Retrieved from http://

www.dailymail.co.uk/tvshowbiz/article-1350685/Kim-Kardashian-reveals-Piers-Morgan-funds-mother-Kris-church.html

Marshall, H., Stuart, J. and Jaunzens, T. (2010). Community organizing goes green. *Social Policy, 39* (4), 8-10.

Marshall, P. D. (1997). *Celebrity and power: Fame in contemporary culture*. Minneapolis, MN: University of Minnesota Press.

Marshall, P. D. (2010). The promotion and presentation of the self: Celebrity as marker of presentational media. *Celebrity Studies, 1(1),* 35-48.

Martin, M. (2011, August 23.) Beauty shop: DSK, Kardashian, and Colombiana. [Radio Broadcast]. *Tell Me More*. New York: NPR. Transcript retrieved from the Newspapers Plus database.

Marwick, A. and boyd, d. (2010). I tweet honestly, I tweet passionately: Twitter users, context collapse, and the imagined audience. *New Media and Society*, Retrieved from http://www.tiara.org/blog/wp-content/uploads/2010/07/marwick_boyd_twitter_nms.pdf.

Marwick, A. and boyd, d. (2011). To see and be seen: Celebrity practice on Twitter. *Convergence: The International Journal of Research into New Media Technologies 17* (2), 139-158. Retrieved from http://www.tiara.org/blog/wp-content/uploads/2011/07/marwick_boyd_to_see_and_be_seen.pdf.

McClain, A. (2010). From Wordnerds to the Aussie Posse: Collective identity on the *American Idol* message boards. In L. Baruh and J. H. Park (Eds.), *Reel politics: reality television as a platform for political discourse* (pp. 134-150). Newcastle upon Tyne, United Kingdom: Cambridge Scholars Publishing.

McClain, A. (2011). *American ideal: How American Idol constructs celebrity, collective identity, and American discourses*. Lanham, MD: Lexington Books.

McFadden, C. (Writer), (2010, May 24). Kardashians [Television series episode]. In J. Condon (Executive Producer), Nightline. New York, New York: ABC.

McKay, H. (2012, January 12). When celebs auction their stuff for charity, they often keep most of the profits. *Fox News*. Retrieved from http://www.foxnews.com/entertainment/2012/01/12/when-celebs-auction-their-stuff-for-charity-often-keep-most-profits/#ixzz1jMDllSBb.

McRobbie, A. (2004): Post-feminism and popular culture. *Feminist Media Studies, 4,* 255-264.

McRobbie, A. (2009). *The aftermath of feminism*. Los Angeles: Sage.

Meehan, E. (2005). *Why TV is not our fault*. New York: Rowman & Littlefield.

Merkin, D. (2010, December 4). The wild bunch. *The New York Times*. Retrieved from http://tmagazine.blogs.nytimes.com/2010/12/04/the-wild-bunch.

Mirage hotel and casino. (2012, June 6). Retrieved from www.mirage.com.

Mittell, J. (2007). Film and television narrative. In D. Herman (Ed.), *The Cambridge companion to narrative* (pp. 155-171). New York: Cambridge University Press.

Money, B., Shimp, T., and Sakano, T. (2006). Celebrity endorsements in Japan and the United States: Is negative information all that harmful? *Journal of Advertising Research, 46* (1), 113-23.

Moran, J. (2000). *Star authors: Literary celebrity in America*. London: Pluto Press.

Morgan, P. (2011, January 30). Piers Morgan the Insider. *Mail on Sunday*. Retrieved from the Newspapers Plus database.

Morozov, E. (2009). Iran: Downside to the " Twitter Revolution." *Dissent, 56* (4), 10-14.

Mungiu-Pippidi, A. and Munteanu, I. (2009). Moldova's Twitter revolution. *Journal of Democracy, 20* (3), 136-142.

Muntean, N. and Petersen, A.H. (2009). Celebrity Twitter: Strategies of intrusions and disclosure in the age of technoculture. *M/C Journal, 12* (5). Retrieved from http://www.journal.mediaculture.org.au/index.php/mcjournal/article/viewArticle/194.

Murray, L. (2012). Teen upbeat despite missing date with Taylor Swift. *USA Today*. Retrieved from http://www.usatoday.com/life/music/awards/story/2012-04-02/taylor-swift-teen-with-cancer/53940758/1

Napoli, P. (2010). Revisiting "mass communication" and the "work" of the audience in the new media environment. *Media, Culture and Society, 32* (3), 505-516.

Newcomb, H. (1988). One night of prime time. In J. Carey (Ed.), *Media, myths, and narrative* (88-112). Beverly Hills, CA: Sage Publications.

Newman, J. and Bruce, L. (2011, February 16). How the Kardashians made $65 million last year. *The Hollywood Reporter*. Retrieved from http://www.hollywood reporter.com/news/how-kardashians-made-65-million-100349.

Nip, J. (2004). The relationship between online and offline communities: The case of the queer sisters. *Media, Culture & Society, 26* (3), 409-428.

Novel idea: Fans get to name Kardashian book. (2011, May 24). *The Associated Press*. Retrieved from the Newspapers Plus database.

O'Dell, J. (2010, October 1). Influence versus popularity on Twitter: Kim Kardashian case study. *Mashable.com*. Retrieved from http://mashable.com/2010/10/01/twitter-kim-kardashian/

O'Leary, K. (2010, August 23). "Sisters torn apart," *US Weekly*, 42-47.

Orenstein, H. (2012, August 1). Kendall and Kylie Jenner: Stylish sisters cover "Seventeen," talk spin-off. *The Huffington Post*. Retrieved, from http://www.huffingtonpost.com/2012/07/31/kendall-and-kylie-jenner-_n_1725644.html

Ostrow, A. (2009, April 28). How many people actually use Twitter? *Mashable.com*. Retrieved from http://mashable.com/2009/04/28/twitter-active-users.

Ouelette, L. & Murray, S. (2009). Introduction. In S. Murray and L. Ouellette (Eds.), *Reality TV: Remaking television culture (2nd ed.)* (pp. 1–20). New York: New York University Press.

Page, R. (2007). Gender. In D. Herman (Ed.), *The Cambridge companion to narrative* (pp. 189-202). New York: Cambridge University Press.

Papacharissi, Z. & de Fatima Oliveira, M. (2012). Affective news and networked publics: The rhythms of news storytelling on #Egypt. *Journal of Communication 62* (2), 266–282.

Pear Analytics. (2009). Twitter Study – August 2009. Retrieved September 11, 2013 from http://www.pearanalytics.com/wp-content/uploads/2012/12/Twitter-Study-August-2009.pdf.

Perez-Feria, R. (2011, May 16). Kardashian, Inc. *The Las Vegas Sun*. Retrieved from the Newspapers Plus database.

Piazza, J. (2011). *Celebrity, Inc*. New York: Open Road Integrated Media.

Piazza, J. (2012, January 28). How much can a celebrity make for tweeting? *New York Times Magazine*. Retrieved from http://www.vulture.com/2012/01/how-much-can-a-celebrity-make-for-tweeting.html.

Phelan, J. (2007). Rhetoric/Ethics. In D. Herman (Ed.), *The Cambridge Companion to Narrative* (pp. 203-216). New York: Cambridge University Press.

Popularity reigns supreme. (2011, October 30). *The Sunday Times (Perth)*. Retrieved from the Newspapers Plus database.

Pozner, J. (2004, Fall). The unreal world. *Ms*. Pp. 50-53.

Pozner, J. (2010). *Reality bites back*. Berkeley, CA: Seal Press.

Primis, A. (2011, October 27). Fruit of the land. *The Philadelphia Inquirer*. Retrieved from the Newspapers Plus database.

Puente, M. (2011, November 1). What's next for the Kardashian brand? *USA Today*. Retrieved from the Newspapers Plus database.

Raphael, C. (2009). The political economic origins of reali-TV. In S. Murray and L. Ouellette (Eds.), *Reality TV: Remaking television culture (2nd ed.)* (pp. 123-140). New York: New York University Press.

Redmond, S. (2006). Intimate fame everywhere. In S. Holmes and S. Redmond (Eds.), *Framing celebrity: New directions in celebrity culture* (pp. 27-44). New York: Routledge.

Rein, I., Kotler, P., and Stoller, M. (1997). *High Visibility*. New York: Dodd, Mead, and Co.

Reines, R. (2011, November 3). Sophie's new choice. *The Sunday Telegraph (Sydney)*. Retrieved from the Newspapers Plus database.

Reinstein, M. (2010, August 30). Why Paris hates Kim. *US Weekly, 811*, 46-47.

Rexrode, C. (2011, November 3). Twitter changes business of celebrity endorsements. *The Associated Press.* Retrieved from the Newspapers Plus database.

Rice, L. (2010, August 30). 'Keeping Up with the Kardashians' premiere attracts record audience. *Entertainment Weekly.* Retrieved from http://insidetv.ew.com/2010/08/23/keeping-up-with-the-kardashian-return-attracts-record-audience/.

Rich, A. (1994). Compulsory heterosexuality and lesbian existence. In *Blood, Bread, and Poetry.* Norton Paperback: New York. (Original work published 1980).

Ritchie, R. (2011, January 1). More Bad Hair Days. *The Sunday Telegraph (Sydney).* Retrieved from the Newspapers Plus database.

Roberts, R. (Writer). (2011, June 6). Reality TV superstars. [Television Broadcast]. *Good Morning America.* New York: ABC. Transcript retrieved from the Newspapers Plus database.

Rojek, C. (2001) *Celebrity.* London: Reaktion.

Ross, R. (2010, December 16). Kris Jenner embarks on joint venture with Music Management Group. Retrieved from http://www.tvguide.com/News/Kris-Jenner-Music-1026832.aspx.

Schickel, R. (2000). *Intimate strangers: The culture of celebrity in America.* Chicago: Ivan R. Dee.

Separation anxiety haunts Kourtney. (2011, January 13). *The Hamilton Spectator.* Retrieved from the Newspapers Plus database.

Shepatin, M. (2010, July 18). Kim Kardashian's a ca'rear' woman. *NY Post.* Retrieved September 11, 2013 from http://nypost.com/2010/07/18/kim-kardashians-a-carear-woman/.

Sillars, M. & Gronbeck, B. (2001). *Communication criticism: rhetoric, social codes, cultural studies.* Prospect Heights, IL: Waveland Press.

Silverstone, R. (1988). Television myth and culture. In J. Carey (ed.), *Media, myths, and narrative* 20-47). Beverly Hills, CA: Sage Publications.

Singletary, M. (2011, January 13). Dirty money. *The Washington Post.* Retrieved from http://www.washingtonpost.com/wpdyn/content/article/2011/01/13/AR2011011301659.html.

Sisario, B. (2012, July 10). Spin Magazine is sold to Buzzmedia, with plans to expand online reach. *The New York Times.* Retrieved from http://mediadecoder.blogs.nytimes.com/2012/07/10/spin-magazine-being-sold-to-buzzmedia-with-plans-to-expand-online-reach/.

Skeggs, B. & Wood, H. (2012). *Reacting to reality television.* New York: Routledge.

Smith, A. (2010). *8% of online Americans use Twitter.* Washington, DC: Pew Research Center's Internet & American Life Project.

Smith, A. and Brenner, J. (2012). *Twitter use 2012.* Washington, DC: Pew Research Center's Internet & American Life Project.

Spencer, L. (2011, August 19). Kim's all-Star wedding. [Television Broadcast]. *Good Morning America.* New York: ABC. Transcript retrieved from the Newspapers Plus database.

Spurgeon, C. (2008). *Advertising and new media.* New York: Routledge.

Stacy, J. (1994). *Star gazing: Hollywood cinema and female spectatorship.* New York: Routledge.

Stelter, B. (2008, July 8). Whichever screen, people are watching. *The New York Times,* p. C5.

Stelter, B. (2011, November 2). Marriage may end; Wedding went on. *New York Times.* Retrieved from the Newspapers Plus database.

Steyer, J. (2003). *The other parent.* New York: Atria Books.

Stoeffel, K. (2013, January 7). If Kim Kardashian won't sell baby pics, who will? *New York Magazine.* Retrieved from http://nymag.com/thecut/2013/01/kim-kardashian-wont-sell-baby-pics.html.

Teen Choice Award winners. (2011, August 8). *The Associated Press.* Retrieved from the Newspapers Plus database.

Technorati. (2012). State of the blogosphere. Retrieved from http://technorati.com/social-media/article/state-of-the-blogosphere-2011-introduction/.

The Monday File: Reasons to laugh, play and celebrate. (2011, January 17). *The Hamilton Spectator.* Retrieved from the Newspapers Plus database.

Thompson, K. (2003). *Storytelling in film and television*. Cambridge, MA: Harvard University Press.

Thorburn. (1988). Television as an aesthetic medium. In J. Carey (Ed.), *Media, myths, and narrative* (48–66). Beverly Hills, CA: Sage Publications.

Thurlow, C. & Mroczek, K. (2011). Introduction: Fresh perspectives on new media sociolingustics. In C. Thurlow & K. Mroczek (Eds.), *Digital discourse* (pp. xix-xliv). New York: Oxford University Press.

Time Warner Senior Corporate Executives, (2012). Retrieved from http://www.timewarner.com/our-company/management/senior-corporate-executives/.

Tran, K. (2012a, August 13). Kardashians to launch brand overseas. *Women's Wear Daily*. Retrieved from http://www.wwd.com/retail-news/people/kardashians-to-launch-brand-overseas-6160177?module=hp-hero-topstories.

Tran, K. (2012b, October 15). Jenner Girls to Launch Juniors Line. *Women's Wear Daily*. Retrieved from http://www.wwd.com/fashion-news/fashion-scoops/jenner-girls-in-juniors-fashion-6407912?src=nl/mornReport/20121015.

Tschorn, A. (February 26, 2010) Kardashian endorsements seem to have va-va-vroom. *Los Angeles Times*. Retrieved from http://latimesblogs.latimes.com/alltherage/2010/02/kim-kardashian-and-products-endorsements-perfume-nascar-cupcakes-candles-and-more.html.

The Twitaholic.com top 100 twitterholics based on followers. (October 9, 2012). Retrieved from http://twitaholic.com/.

Tuchman, G. (1978). The symbolic annihilation of women in mass media. In G. Tuchman, A. Daniels, & J. Benet. (Eds.), *Hearth and home: Images of women in mass media* (pp. 3-38). New York: Oxford University Press.

Tuchman, G., Daniels, A., & Benet, J. (1978). (Eds.), *Hearth and home: Images of women in mass media*. New York: Oxford University Press.

Tucker-Evans, A. (2011, January 9). Small slice of eleven. *The Sunday Mail (Brisbane)*. Retrieved from the Newspapers Plus database.

Turner, G., Bonner, F., and Marshal, P.D. (2000). *Fame games: The production of celebrity in Australia*. Melbourne: Cambridge University Press.

Turner, G. (2004). *Understanding celebrity*. Thousand Oaks, CA: Sage.

Twitchell, J. (1999). *Lead us into temptation: The triumph of American materialism*. New York: Columbia University Press.

Veblen, T. (1899/1994). *The Theory of the Leisure Class*. New York: Dover Publications.

Villareal, Y. (2012, April 24). Kardashian family signs 3-year deal with E! network. *Los Angeles Times*. Retrieved from http://latimesblogs.latimes.com/showtracker/2012/04/kardashian-family-signs-3-year-deal-with-e-network.html.

Villarreal, Y. and Tschorn, A. (2011, November 27). Will Kardashians ever krumble? *The Los Angeles Times*. Retrieved from the Newspapers Plus database.

Vossen, G. & Hagemann, S. (2007). *Unleashing web 2.0: From concepts to creativity*. New York: Morgan Kaufmann Publishers.

Walsh, J. & Ward, L. (2008). Adolescent gender role portrayals in the media: 1950s to present. In P.E. Jamieson & D. Romer (Eds.), *The changing portrayals of adolescents in the media since 1950* (p. 132-164). New York: Oxford University Press.

Walters, B. (2011, December 14.) The 10 most fascinating people of 2011. [Television Broadcast]. *News Special Report*. New York: ABC. Transcript retrieved from the Newspapers Plus database.

Walton, S. & Jaffe, A. (2011). "Stuff White people like": Stance, class, race, and Internet commentary (pp. 199-219). In C. Thurlow & K. Mroczek (Eds.), *Digital discourse*. New York: Oxford University Press.

Wasserman, T. (2012, January 12). Facebook to Hit 1 Billion User Mark in August. *Mashable.com*. Retrieved from http://mashable.com/2012/01/12/facebook-1-billion-users/.

Watts, A. (2008). The search for authentic self in reality-TV Celebrity. In K. R. Hart (Ed.), *Film and television stardom* (pp. 236-267). Newcastle upon Tyne, United Kingdom: Cambridge Scholars Publishing.

Weber, B. (2009). *Makeover TV: Selfhood, citizenship, and celebrity*. Durham, NC: Duke University Press Books.

Wheeler, K. (2011, January 25). "Kourtney & Kim Take New York" debuts with huge ratings -
- 3 million viewers. *Examiner.com*. Retrieved from http://www.examiner.com/tv-in-
national/kourtney-kim-take-new-york-debuts-with-huge-ratings-3-million-viewers.

White, H. (1987). *The content of the form: Narrative discourse and historical representation.*
Baltimore, MD: Johns Hopkins University Press.

Who owns what. (2012, May 15). *Columbia Journalism Review.* Retrieved from www.cjr.org/
resources.

Williamson, J. (1978). *Decoding advertisements.* London: Marion Boyars.

Wilson, E. (2010, November 17). Kim Kardashian Inc. *The New York Times.* Retrieved from
http://www.nytimes.com/2010/11/18/fashion/18KIM.html?emc=eta1.

Wood, J. (2011). *Gendered lives: Communication, gender, and culture* (9th. ed). Boston:
Wadsworth Cengage Learning.

Xifra, J. and Grau, F. (2010). Nanoblogging PR: The discourse on public relations in Twitter.
Public Relations Review, 36 (2), 171-174.

Zelizer, B. (1997). Has communication explained journalism? In D. Berkowitz (ed.), *Social
meanings of news* (pp. 23-30). Thousand Oaks, CA: Sage.

Index

About the Author

Amanda Scheiner McClain is assistant professor of communications and coordinator of arts and communications at Holy Family University in Philadelphia, PA. McClain earned her doctorate in Mass Media and Communication from Temple University. Her first book, *American Ideal: How* American Idol *Constructs Celebrity, Collective Identity, and American Discourses*, was published by Lexington Books in 2011. McClain has presented research at many national conferences, including the Association for Education in Journalism and Mass Communication, the National Communication Association, and the Popular Culture Association/American Culture Association (PCA/ACA). She is Television Studies Co-Chair for the PCA/ACA and Television Studies Chair for the Mid-Atlantic Popular & American Culture Association. McClain's research interests include reality TV, social media, celebrity, narrative, and media representations of women.

Lightning Source UK Ltd.
Milton Keynes UK
UKHW021259140223
416998UK00037B/695